AQA Psycholo

Exclusively endorsed by AQA

AS

Psychology

Revision Guide

Julia Willerton

Jane Willson

Simon Green

Nelson Thornes

Published in 2011 by:
Nelson Thornes Ltd
Delta Place
27 Bath Road
CHELTENHAM
GL53 7TH
United Kingdom

11 12 13 14 15 / 10 9 8 7 6 5 4 3 2 1

A catalogue record for this book is available from the British Library

ISBN 978 1 4085 0816 9

Cover photograph: Christoph Wilhelm/Getty Images

Page make-up by Pantek Arts Ltd, Maidstone

Printed and bound in Spain by GraphyCems

In memory of our colleague and friend, Jane Willson

Contents

Unit 2 Biological Psychology, Social Psychology and Individual Differences

Introduction

This revision guide will provide you with the essentials of revision.

You will also find some practical advice in this guide about how to apply your knowledge of improving memory to help you to recall in the exam what you have revised.

The answers to the quick text questions at the end of each chapter can be found at www.nelsonthornes.com/psychology_answers.

What you will be asked to do in the exam

In the exams you will be asked to show your knowledge and understanding of psychological concepts, theories and research studies. You will also be asked to evaluate theories and studies and to apply your knowledge to situations or scenarios. Examination questions come in a range of different formats and styles to test each of these skills. Working out exactly what the question is asking you to do is the first step towards getting good marks in the exam.

Injunction words and their interpretation

Injunction	The examiner wants you to …
Outline two factors that cause stress in the workplace	Give a brief description or overview of two things that lead to stress at work
Describe strategies for memory improvement	Give details of each step or stage applied in key methods used to improve memory. Provide enough detail so that someone could carry out the process
Explain how locus of control influences independent behaviour	Give details of the way internal locus of control influences people to act independently and the way external locus of control affects independent behaviour
Justify your choice of sampling method	Explain why you have chosen a sampling method, referring to its strengths
Evaluate the behavioural approach to psychopathology	Talk about the strengths and weaknesses of the behavioural approach to psychopathology. Say how valuable the approach is in understanding mental illness
Identify two characteristics of a securely attached child	Give the name of two of the signs that show a child has a secure attachment

Start by checking that you know the meaning of the 'injunction' (instruction) words used in questions.

When presented with a question, try to pick out the injunction (action) and the topic (target) and so work out what the examiner wants you to do.

How much you need to write

You can tell how much you need to write by looking at the injunction words used in the question and by considering the number of marks awarded for the answer. A question that asks for a 2-mark outline requires less depth and detail than a 6-mark description or a 12-mark question that asks you to describe and evaluate. The same topic (e.g. obedience or workplace stress) could be set as a 2-, 4-, 8- or 12-mark question, requiring you to use your knowledge in different ways.

Example exam-style questions

1   Outline two explanations of obedience.
    (2 + 2 marks)

2   When a police officer is wearing a uniform and directing traffic, you are very likely to obey them. However, if you meet the same police officer but they are dressed in civilian clothes, you are less likely to obey them. Using your knowledge of obedience, explain why you are less likely to obey the plain-clothes officer.
    (4 marks)

3   Describe and evaluate explanations of obedience.   *(12 marks)*

Tackling different kinds of questions

Knowledge-based questions

These questions ask you to demonstrate your knowledge of a psychological theory, explanation or model (e.g. example question 1). To answer this kind of question you need to be able to summarise explanations and theories clearly in your own words, drawing on the most important points. For a 2-mark question you need to select the most important points to include, but for a 6-mark question you may be able to cover all of the main features. Knowledge-based questions are often worth 4 or 6 marks and a good way to revise is to practise summarising key theories, models or explanations giving sufficient detail for 4 or 6 marks.

Application-based (scenario) questions

This kind of question asks you to apply your knowledge of psychology to a situation, or something that could happen in real life. This type of question could be asked about any of the topics. These questions are unpredictable but they are easy to tackle if you do this in a systematic way. Using example question 2.

- **Step 1: Look for the clues in the scenario.** Application questions contain clues to direct you to the best material to draw on. It may help to underline key words or clues.

- **Step 2: Decide which material is most relevant to use.** Look at the words/sentences you have underlined and think how they relate to theories, studies and ideas about the topic. In example question 2, think about explanations of why people may be more likely to obey a person who is clearly a figure of authority (as shown by their uniform) and less likely to obey someone who does not have the same authority. You don't have to refer to a research study, but if you can identify a relevant study (e.g. Bickman's field experiment here) you must apply it to the scenario rather than simply describe it.

- **Step 3: Refer back to the scenario when writing your answer.** Construct your answer to the question using the material you have selected. It is a good idea to start by referring to the scenario and refer back to it in the middle and at the end of your answer.

Research methods questions

Both exams will include questions that ask you to show your understanding of research methods. These will be short questions and will focus on research studies relating to the topics you have covered. You can prepare for questions about research methods by identifying the method used and spotting the IV and DV in each research study as you revise it.

Essay-style questions

On each of the AS exam papers you will be asked to write one or more extended pieces of writing, often known as mini essays. These can be worth 8, 10 or 12 marks, so look carefully at the number of marks available to decide how much to write. Your performance on longer questions can make a substantial difference to your overall grade, so practise writing mini essays as preparation for your exams.

Mini essays ask you to demonstrate your skills of analysis and evaluation. About half of the marks are awarded for evaluation, so aim to spend about the same amount of time writing the description and evaluation sections of your essay. These do not have to be separated into different sections and a good answer may naturally integrate the description and evaluation.

Evaluating theories or explanations

These can be effectively evaluated by considering evidence that supports or contradicts the claims made. You can also evaluate theories by considering their relevance or importance in daily life or discussing how they apply to real-life situations or problems. This kind of evaluation is known as commentary and can be very effective.

Evaluating research studies

These can be evaluated in terms of their methodology and their ethical issues. Remember to consider strengths as well as weaknesses of research studies. Depending on the relevance to the question, you may talk about the method used (for example, an observation or a laboratory experiment) and refer to ideas such as control, validity, replication, the sample of people studied and the existence of possible confounding variables. You can also evaluate research studies by considering the implications of the findings. For example, if eyewitness accounts were found to be inaccurate, this would have implications for court cases and criminal trials.

The quality of your written communication (QWC) will be assessed, so make sure that you write in legible sentences.

Cognitive psychology

Models of memory

The multi-store model

> **You need to know how to**
>
> ✔ describe the components and processes of the multi-store model (MSM)
>
> ✔ describe and explain the concepts of encoding, duration and capacity
>
> ✔ describe and use research studies to evaluate the model
>
> ✔ explain the strengths and weaknesses of the model.

The multi-store model (MSM) of memory (Atkinson and Shiffrin, 1968)

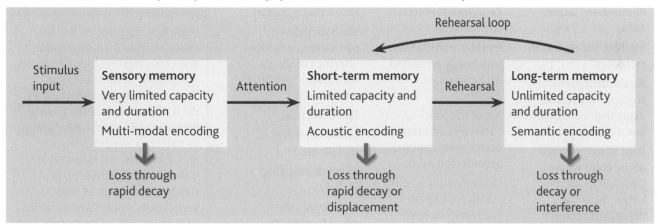

Checklist for describing the MSM

- There are three separate stores – sensory, short-term (STM) and long-term (LTM).
- Sensory memory has a store for each of the senses, e.g. hearing, vision, touch.
- STM and LTM are unitary stores – each operates like a single unit with no separate compartments.
- Information:
  - entering the memory system passes through the stores in a fixed sequence
  - can be lost at any stage
  - usually has to be recoded as it passes from store to store
  - can only pass from sensory memory to STM if given attention
  - if not given attention is lost (through decay)
  - can only pass from STM to LTM if we rehearse (repeat) it
  - if not rehearsed enough, it is lost (through decay and displacement).
- Each store is different in terms of encoding, duration and capacity.

Think about it

Try to understand what happens at each stage of the memory process and why, rather than simply learn the diagram by rote. You will remember the details much better in the exam if you really understand the model.

Capacity, duration and encoding

The components of the multi-store model differ in three important ways. The following tables summarise their qualities, how they have been investigated by researchers, and what that research tells us.

Summary descriptions of the terms used to describe memory

Capacity	Duration	Encoding
Space – amount of information that can be stored in memory at any one time.	**Time** – the length of time that memories can be held.	**Format** – the way in which information is represented in memory, e.g. by sound, meaning or image.

How researchers have investigated capacity, duration and encoding in STM

Capacity	Duration	Encoding
Researchers: Jacobs; Miller	Researchers: Peterson and Peterson	Researchers: Conrad
Method: the digit span technique.	Method: participants very briefly presented with consonant trigram.	Method: showed participants a random sequence of six consonants very briefly on a screen.
Participants given strings of unrelated digits that increase by one digit every time.	Asked to count backwards in threes from a given digit (to prevent rehearsal).	Two conditions: similar sounding (B, T, D, etc.) different sounding (Y, R, F)
Digit span measured at the point where participants can no longer recall the digits in the correct sequence.	On each trial (i.e. with a different trigram each time) stopped after an interval ranging between three and 18 seconds and asked to recall the trigram correctly.	Participants then asked to write the consonants down in the correct order.

What they found

STM capacity is very limited. Digit span is 7+ or −2. Span can be increased by chunking, i.e. by putting several items into a meaningful 'chunk'.	STM has very brief duration when rehearsal is prevented. Participants could recall about 80 per cent of the trigrams correctly after three seconds but fewer than 10 per cent after 18 seconds.	STM uses mainly acoustic coding. Participants found it more difficult to recall and made more errors on the lists of similar-sounding consonants.

AQA Examiner's tip

You must know the characteristics of sensory memory so that you can describe the MSM: **Capacity** – very limited (about 9–10 items in visual sensory memory). Items fade away rapidly (within about 0.5 seconds for visual items and about 2 seconds for heard items) so **duration** is extremely limited. Sensory memory can receive information from all of the senses, e.g. vision, hearing, smell and touch so **encoding** is multi-modal. However, the main feature of the MSM is the distinction between STM and LTM, and most research has focused on these two stores.

Think about it

Learn one study for each of the characteristics (capacity, duration and encoding) in reasonable detail. Try to really understand what the researchers did and why they did it. For example, Peterson and Peterson used consonant trigrams so that they were meaningless and, therefore, not memorable. If they had used three-letter combinations, such as 'CUP', participants would have found it easy to recall even if rehearsal had been prevented. Why do you think they chose the backwards counting task to prevent rehearsal?

Think about it

Why did Conrad present the consonants visually instead of saying them out loud and ask participants to write them down rather than say them out loud?

Discussion points

Digit span is an artificial measure – not a real-life situation.

No independent measure of a 'chunk'. Number of chunks we can recall depends on various factors, e.g. the number of items within a chunk, the anxiety of participants.

Baddeley and others have found that we can recall from STM as many items as we can pronounce in about two seconds, so capacity might be better measured in terms of pronunciation time rather than number of items.

It is hard in experiments to exclude the influence of LTM.

Research is based on artificial stimuli like trigrams – not real life.

Peterson technique might not be an accurate measure of duration because:

- counting backwards in threes was used to prevent rehearsal, but it might have actually displaced the trigram
- participants had to carry out several trials. Accuracy of recall became worse as the trials went on. It might be that trigrams presented early on caused confusion for later trigrams.

Amount of information seems to be crucial. A single three-letter word, e.g. DOG, can be recalled easily after 18 seconds without rehearsal, but a three-letter nonsense trigram, e.g. QKM, cannot.

Research used artificial stimuli – not real life.

Conrad used university students as his participants – might not be a representative sample.

Conrad used consonants – these can only be represented in acoustic or visual code so he was not able to rule out semantic coding as a method of encoding in STM.

However, Baddeley carried out a similar study using words and concluded that Conrad's findings were correct, i.e. acoustic coding is the preferred method of encoding in STM.

How researchers have investigated capacity, duration and encoding in LTM

It is accepted by researchers that LTM has unlimited capacity so it is impossible to carry out research into capacity.

Duration

Researchers, e.g. Bahrick

Tested nearly 400 American high-school graduates on their memory for former schoolmates

Used a variety of memory tests – recognition of photos, matching names to photos and recalling names with no photo cue

---

Encoding

Researchers, e.g. Baddeley

Constructed lists of words in four categories: (1) sound similar, (2) do not sound similar, (3) mean the same, (4) do not mean the same

Presented 10 words from each list to participants

After each presentation, prevented rehearsal.

Recall was tested after 20 minutes.

What they found

Participants performed well up to 34 years after they had left high school.

Memory performance was generally better on recognition tasks than recall tasks.

Performance declined after 47 years.

Participants performed least well on the lists where the words were similar in meaning.

Baddeley concluded that this was because LTM codes for meaning (semantically).

Discussion points

The study looked at how memory works in real life not in laboratory settings.

It is difficult to control extraneous variables when investigating duration of LTM.

Information in LTM can last for a lifetime, but it sometimes needs retrieval cues to get to it.

Later research suggests that information lasts longer if it is very well processed and if the material is thoroughly understood rather than learned by rote.

This study used real words rather than meaningless consonants, but it was still carried out in a laboratory and so was artificial. This reduces the validity.

We can instantly recognise sounds like police sirens – suggests that we can code acoustically in LTM as well.

Other research evidence suggests, although semantic encoding is the preferred form, we can code visually (by imagery) in LTM as well.

Strengths and weaknesses of the multi-store model

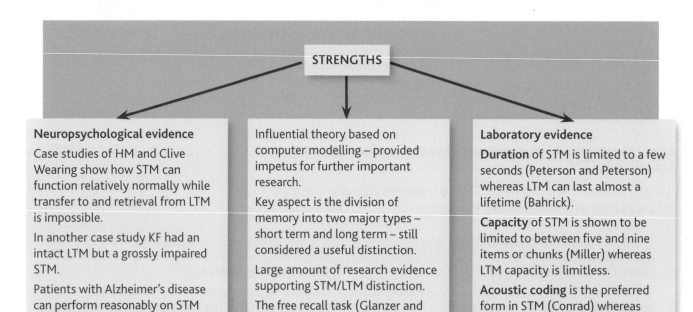

STRENGTHS

Neuropsychological evidence

Case studies of HM and Clive Wearing show how STM can function relatively normally while transfer to and retrieval from LTM is impossible.

In another case study KF had an intact LTM but a grossly impaired STM.

Patients with Alzheimer's disease can perform reasonably on STM tasks but not on LTM tasks.

Brain scanning techniques have shown different areas of the brain activated in STM and LTM tasks.

Influential theory based on computer modelling – provided impetus for further important research.

Key aspect is the division of memory into two major types – short term and long term – still considered a useful distinction.

Large amount of research evidence supporting STM/LTM distinction.

The free recall task (Glanzer and Cunitz) shows how STM and LTM function differently. It also supports the MSM in showing how rehearsal moves information from STM to LTM.

Laboratory evidence

Duration of STM is limited to a few seconds (Peterson and Peterson) whereas LTM can last almost a lifetime (Bahrick).

Capacity of STM is shown to be limited to between five and nine items or chunks (Miller) whereas LTM capacity is limitless.

Acoustic coding is the preferred form in STM (Conrad) whereas semantic coding is the preferred form in LTM (Baddeley).

Examiner's tip

You may be asked to describe and evaluate the MSM for 12 marks. You only have 6 marks for evaluation, so choose a few key points that you can elaborate on. You don't need to include strengths and weaknesses, but your answer will be more balanced if you do. You could also be asked to apply the model or use knowledge of the model to explain something. For example, you may be given a case study of someone with impared memory and be asked to explain whether it supports the model and why.

Think about it

What extraneous variables might have posed problems in Bahrick's research?

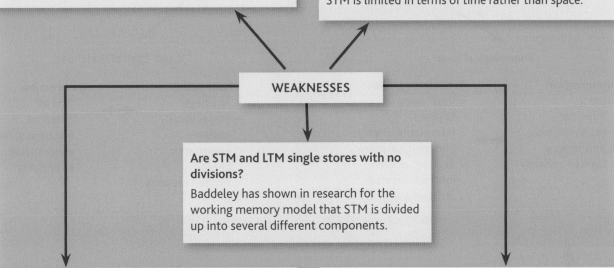

Is rehearsal the only way of getting information into LTM?

KF could put new information into LTM even though his STM was not working properly – there must be some other route into LTM.

Memories for shocking events have been shown to imprint directly into LTM without rehearsal.

There are many techniques to improve memory that do not depend on rehearsal.

Are there different ways of interpreting research studies?

KF can be used to support the model or cast doubt on it, as he can put items into LTM without processing them in STM first.

Digit span is about seven items. Miller thought this was because we only have this amount of space in STM. Baddeley thought it was because we can only remember as many items as we can say in about two seconds, i.e. STM is limited in terms of time rather than space.

WEAKNESSES

Are STM and LTM single stores with no divisions?

Baddeley has shown in research for the working memory model that STM is divided up into several different components.

Does information flow through the system in a fixed sequence?

Information from LTM sometimes has to be activated before the final stages of processing in STM can occur, e.g. you need to get the pronunciation for the letter 'B' from LTM before you can convert its visual image into an acoustic code in STM.

Is human memory that simple?

The MSM is too simple – it cannot explain why we remember some things better than others or why recognition is easier than recall, for example.

The working memory model (WM)

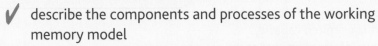

You need to know how to

✔ describe the components and processes of the working memory model

✔ use research studies to evaluate the model

✔ explain the strengths and weaknesses of the model.

AQA Examiner's tip

This is a model of short-term memory. If you are asked to give a criticism of the model, remember that it is inappropriate to 'blame' the researchers for not explaining LTM. That is like criticising an orange for not being an apple!

Working memory model

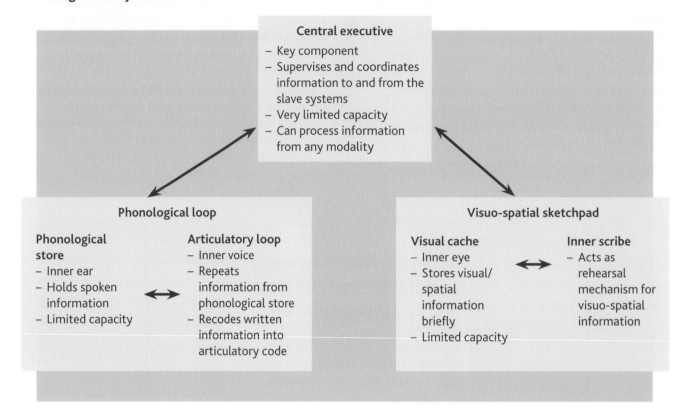

Checklist for describing the working memory model

- ■ It explains how short-term memory works.
- ■ It consists of several different components (STM is not unitary as in the MSM).
- ■ Each component has a particular function – includes not only storage but manipulation and analysis of information.
- ■ Central executive is the key component that oversees and coordinates the other components (slave systems).
- ■ There is a two-way flow of information between the central executive and the slave systems.
- ■ The slave systems have separate responsibilities and work independently of one another.
- ■ The phonological loop is subdivided into the phonological store (inner ear) and the articulatory loop (inner voice). It is a limited capacity, temporary storage system for holding auditory information in speech-based form.
- ■ The visuo-spatial sketchpad (inner eye) is subdivided into the visual cache and the inner scribe. It is a limited capacity, temporary storage system for holding visual and spatial information.
- ■ The model has been modified over the years to take account of research findings, and new components have been added.

How have researchers investigated working memory?

Researchers have made use of the dual task technique to provide evidence for the distinction between components.

Summary of supporting research

What they did	What they found	Discussion points
Baddeley and Hitch (1974) Gave participants a dual task: ■ a reasoning task ■ reading aloud	Participants could do both tasks very well simultaneously.	STM must have different components that can process more than one type of information at a time.
Baddeley *et al.* (1975) Gave participants brief visual presentations of lists of words, either short words or long words, and asked participants to recall the list immediately in correct serial order.	Participants could recall more short words than long words (word length effect).	Concluded that the loop can hold as many items as can be said in 1.5–2 seconds. So the loop has a time limit rather than being limited by items.
Baddeley *et al.* (1973) Gave participants a dual task to do simultaneously: ■ a tracking task ■ a visual imagery task	Participants were much poorer at the dual task than at each task performed alone.	Concluded that both tasks needed to be done in the visuo-spatial sketch pad so were competing for the same limited resources.

Strengths and weaknesses of the working memory model

Working memory strengths

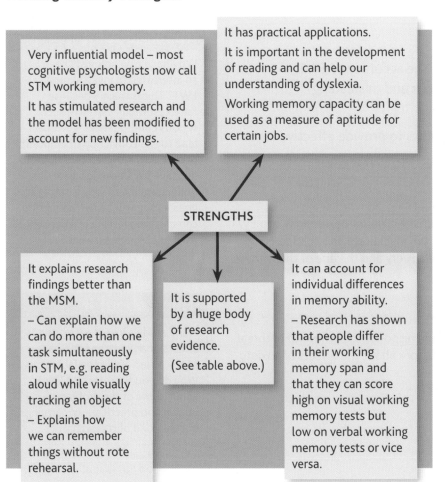

Very influential model – most cognitive psychologists now call STM working memory.

It has stimulated research and the model has been modified to account for new findings.

It has practical applications.

It is important in the development of reading and can help our understanding of dyslexia.

Working memory capacity can be used as a measure of aptitude for certain jobs.

STRENGTHS

It explains research findings better than the MSM.

– Can explain how we can do more than one task simultaneously in STM, e.g. reading aloud while visually tracking an object

– Explains how we can remember things without rote rehearsal.

It is supported by a huge body of research evidence.

(See table above.)

It can account for individual differences in memory ability.

– Research has shown that people differ in their working memory span and that they can score high on visual working memory tests but low on verbal working memory tests or vice versa.

Think about it

Remember KF, whose memory performance can be used to both support and criticise the MSM? You could also use this case study to support the WMM. KF had very impaired digit span but was able to process and recall visual information from STM. This suggests that STM has different components which handle verbal and visual information independently.

Working memory weaknesses

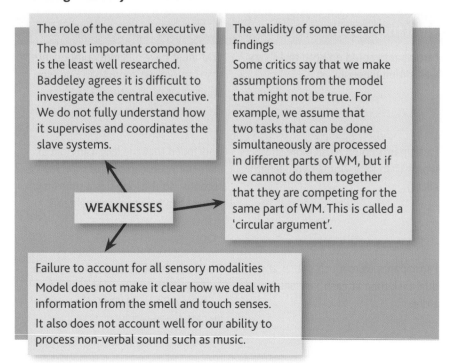

The role of the central executive

The most important component is the least well researched. Baddeley agrees it is difficult to investigate the central executive. We do not fully understand how it supervises and coordinates the slave systems.

The validity of some research findings

Some critics say that we make assumptions from the model that might not be true. For example, we assume that two tasks that can be done simultaneously are processed in different parts of WM, but if we cannot do them together that they are competing for the same part of WM. This is called a 'circular argument'.

WEAKNESSES

Failure to account for all sensory modalities

Model does not make it clear how we deal with information from the smell and touch senses.

It also does not account well for our ability to process non-verbal sound such as music.

Memory in everyday life

Eyewitness testimony (EWT)

You need to know how to

 explain factors that influence the accuracy of EWT, including anxiety, age of witness and misleading information

 describe and use research studies to provide effective commentary.

Over the last 30 years, there has been a huge amount of research into EWT. One of the key findings is that EWT is often inaccurate and is affected by various factors. Two such factors are the *anxiety* and the *age* of the witness.

Anxiety

Anxiety is a state of heightened arousal in response to some kind of threat or danger. Research evidence is contradictory about the effects of anxiety on the accuracy of witness recall.

Think about it

Why have psychologists been so interested in investigating EWT? This is mainly because false testimony can have such serious consequences, i.e. it can lead to the conviction of innocent people. Any research that helps to improve EWT or to increase our understanding of why it sometimes goes wrong will be beneficial. You can use this kind of commentary as AO2 in 12-mark answers.

Think about it

Many studies investigating the effects of anxiety on EWT have been carried out in the laboratory. Why do you think this is? Think about some of the problems – ethical and practical – of carrying out this kind of research.

How researchers have investigated the effects of anxiety on EWT accuracy and what they have found

What they did	What they found	Discussion points
Loftus (1979) Asked participants to sit outside a laboratory where they thought they were listening to a genuine exchange between people inside. Condition 1: overheard a friendly discussion and then saw a man come out of the room with greasy hands holding a pen. Condition 2: overheard a hostile discussion and furniture being overturned and saw a man come out of the room holding a bloodstained knife. Both sets of participants were asked to identify the man from 50 photos.	Participants who had witnessed the more violent scene were less accurate in identifying the man. Loftus concluded that this was because the heightened anxiety of the witnesses in the violent scene caused them to focus on the weapon and not take in other details (weapon effect).	This was a staged experiment, but it was similar to real life in that the participants thought they were waiting to take part in a completely different experiment so were not expecting to be called as a witness. There are ethical issues when participants are unexpectedly exposed to anxiety. The findings of this study have been supported in other research, e.g. Loftus and Christianson (2006) – people who were interviewed six months after seeing a traumatic filmed event could remember the essence of the event very well but had grossly impaired memory of the details surrounding it.
Christianson and Hubinette (1993) Surveyed 110 people who between them had witnessed 22 different bank robberies either as direct victims or as bystanders.	The victims of the crimes who had been subjected to the greatest levels of anxiety were more detailed and accurate in their recall than the bystanders.	This suggests that people react to anxiety-inducing events differently when they occur in real life rather than in a laboratory.

Age of witness

How researchers have investigated the effects of age on EWT accuracy and what they have found

What they did	What they found	Discussion points
Flin et al. (1992) Asked children and adults questions about an incident they had witnessed – one day after the event and then five months after it.	Recall was similar for adults and children after one day but significantly worse for children after a five-month delay.	This decline in accuracy with time is important because court appearances are often a long time after the crime.
Gordon et al. (2001) Reviewed a number of studies of child witnesses.	Although children can recall accurately and in detail, they are more susceptible to misleading information than adults.	Davies (1994) has disputed this. He thinks children can resist misleading information if they are questioned very sensitively.
Yarmey (1984) Showed young and elderly adults a film of a staged event and then asked questions about what they had seen.	Eighty per cent of elderly adults (but only 20 per cent of young adults) failed to mention a key detail (attacker had knife in hand).	This was an artificial situation – it might not reflect how people react to a real-life situation.

Think about it

Although the evidence seems quite strong that elderly adults have poorer recall of events than younger adults, there are always some who recall accurately and are not susceptible to misleading information. This suggests that there are individual differences – some people are just better at recalling accurately than others.

AQA Examiner's tip

Do not simply state that adults have more accurate recall than children. You need to differentiate between young and elderly adults.

Misleading information

Misleading information is usually provided after the event (post-event information) and can distort the original memory of the witness. It is often provided in the form of leading questions.

How researchers have investigated the effects of misleading information on EWT and what they have found

What they did	What they found	Discussion points
Loftus and Palmer (1974) Showed a film of a car accident and then asked questions about it. A crucial question was asked about the speed of the car. All groups were asked the same question but a different verb was used (e.g. hit, smashed, bumped, collided, contacted).	Participants who were asked the 'smashed' question produced by far the highest estimate of speed, while those hearing 'contacted' gave the lowest estimate of speed. A week later, participants in the 'smashed' condition were more likely than other participants to report seeing broken glass at the accident scene even though there was none.	The verb used had significant effect on the speed estimate. It continued to affect recall after a delay of a week, suggesting that the false memory had become permanently lodged in memory. Critics of the study suggested that participants might have been responding to demand characteristics.
Loftus (1975) Showed participants film of events leading up to a car accident. One group was then asked questions consistent with the film. The second group were asked the same questions except for one concerning a barn (there had been no barn in the film).	When recalling the film, 17 per cent of the misled group reported seeing a barn but only 3 per cent of the other group said they had seen it.	Loftus concluded that the misled group had incorporated the false information about the barn into their original memory. NB: Although the result was significant, it is clear that not everybody in the misled group was affected by the post-event information.

AQA Examiner's tip

In a 12-mark question on research into misleading information, it is useful to make the general point that most of these studies use artificial situations that do not accurately mimic real-life conditions. There are also ethical issues involved in showing participants films of accidents or crimes. However, only make this point once – do not repeat the same criticism for every study you write about.

Apply it

Imagine you are asking a witness to describe the appearance of a burglar. An open question would be: 'What was he wearing?' How could you change this into a leading question?

Using the cognitive interview to improve EWT

You need to know how to

✔ describe the various techniques used in the cognitive interview

✔ describe and use research studies to provide effective commentary.

Psychologists have tried to devise ways of improving the accuracy of EWT. One possible method is to change the way police interview witnesses to crimes or accidents.

Fisher *et al.* (1987) studied genuine interviews carried out by experienced police officers in Florida and found:

- questions were brief, direct and closed
- sequencing of questions often did not match the witnesses' own image of the event
- police questioners often interrupted, not allowing witnesses to expand on their answers.

On the basis of this kind of research, Geiselman developed the cognitive interview.

Cognitive interview techniques

Technique	Instructions to witness
Context reinstatement (CR)	Think yourself back to the scene of the event. What were you feeling, what had you just been doing, what was the weather like, who was standing around, etc.?
Report everything (RE)	Report everything you can think of about the event even if it seems trivial – it might have a bearing on the event or trigger your memory of something important.
Recall from changed perspective (CP)	Try to put yourself in the shoes of someone else at the scene and describe it from their point of view.
Recall in reverse order (RO)	Report the details of the event from back to front or start with a particular aspect of the scene and work backwards or forwards from that.

Fisher *et al.* (1987) added some features to make a version called the enhanced cognitive technique – minimal distractions, active listening, ask open-ended questions, pause after each response, avoid interruption, adapt use of language to suit witness and avoid judgemental comments.

How researchers have investigated the effectiveness of the cognitive interview and what they have found

What they did	What they found	Discussion points
Geiselman *et al.* (1985) Showed participants videos of a simulated crime. They tested recall by cognitive interview, standard interview or hypnosis.	Cognitive interview prompted the most information.	However, Koehnken *et al.* (1999) found that it produced more incorrect information than the standard interview.
Fisher *et al.* (1990) Trained real detectives to use enhanced cognitive interview with real crime witnesses.	They found that cognitive interview considerably increased the amount of information recalled compared to standard interviews.	The study used real police officers and crime witnesses so lacked artificiality of some other studies.
Milne and Bull (2002) Tested each of the cognitive interview techniques singly or in combination.	All four techniques used singly produced more information than the standard interview, but CR with RE the most effective combination.	This confirmed the beliefs of the UK police that some techniques are more effective than others.

Strategies for memory improvement

> **You need to know how to**
>
> ✔ describe at least two strategies for memory improvement.

Many mnemonics are based on the principles of organisation and visual imagery. Visual imagery works well because you can use dual encoding – the item is remembered verbally, for example as the word 'glove' and also visually as a pictorial image of a glove. Organisation is important because it can aid understanding.

Examples of mnemonics

Peg-word system	First learn the list of peg words, which each rhyme with a number up to 10, e.g. one is a bun, two is a shoe. Associate each word to be remembered with a peg word. If you want to recall a shopping list make a visual image of the first item, e.g. potatoes, with the first peg word, i.e. bun. The more bizarre the image, the better it will be recalled.	You have to learn the peg-word list first. It is only useful for lists (e.g. shopping lists), and we rarely have to commit such lists to memory.
Method of loci	Think of a familiar route, e.g. a walk around your house, your journey to school. Pick distinct places along the route (as many places as items you need to recall). Associate each item to be recalled with a place on the route. When you come to recall, retrace your route and the item will be recalled.	Same problems exist as above except that this method is slightly more flexible.
Keyword method	Used for learning foreign languages. When you are given a new foreign word to learn, think of a similar-sounding English word and form an image of the two meanings. For example, the German word *igel* (pronounced like 'eagle') means hedgehog. Picture an eagle swooping down to catch a hedgehog.	Keyword has been demonstrated to be very effective in learning foreign words, e.g. Gruneberg and Jacobs (1991). It only helps with learning words not grammar.

Make sure that you give a sensible answer to an applied question. If you are asked for a method to remember people's names, for example, do not choose peg word or method of loci as these methods simply do not work for this. It is better to go for a technique similar to keyword where you think of an associated image. For example: Tom – picture his face on the body of a big tom-cat; Harry – picture him as Harry Potter; Alice – picture her with a wide Alice band in her hair.

Apply it

How might you remember other students in your class called Jim, Winston, April and Jenny?

Verbal mnemonics

These can be used when it is important to recall the order of things. For example, to remember the colours of the rainbow you take the first letter of each colour and make up a sentence where each word starts with that initial letter – Red, Orange, Yellow, Green, Blue, Indigo, Violet becomes Richard Of York Gave Battle In Vain. Rhymes or songs can also be used to recall this type of information, for example, 'thirty days hath September, April, June and November' or to remember how to spell a difficult word, 'i before e except after c'.

Apply it

Can you make up a sentence using the initial letters of the planets in order of their distance from the sun? (Mercury, Venus, Earth, Mars, Jupiter, Saturn, Uranus, Neptune.) It is always better if you make up your own sentence because you are using active processing and making use of material that is meaningful and relevant to you. You could do this with some of the psychology material that you want to remember.

Encoding specificity principle

You recall things better if you have cues available to you that were present when you first learned the material. For example, you recall things better if you are in the same place as where you learned them. This is not always possible, but there is evidence to suggest that just imagining yourself back in the place is a powerful memory cue. Remember that context reinstatement is one of the most successful techniques of the cognitive interview.

Recall seems to be better if you are in the same mood or physical state when you retrieve the memory as when you encode it. But beware, this effect is quite weak, and for well-learned material it does not seem important.

Give yourself some breaks in your revision. Research shows that spaced learning is more effective for long-term retention than cramming all of your revision into one long session.

Active processing

Remember what the MSM says about transferring material from STM to LTM. Simple rote rehearsal can be effective if you have plenty of time to repeat the items and you are not disturbed. However, research has shown that rehearsal is much more effective if it is elaborate. In other words, you need to think about the material to be learned and encode it semantically – this way you set up several associations in LTM and so you have several retrieval routes which will make it easier to recall.

Apply it

You can apply the same sort of principles to writing yourself a set of revision notes. What do you think are the best strategies for you? Think organisation, visual imagery, elaboration, practice.

Using a memory strategy to improve revision

When you are revising from a textbook, try the following PQRST method based on the following three principles:

- organisation
- elaboration
- practice.

PQRST method

Preview

Skim read the chapter paying particular attention to headings and subheadings. You are beginning to organise the material by getting an overview.

Read

Now read the section carefully, checking all the time that you understand what it means. Try to answer the questions you posed in the previous step so that you are doing further elaboration. You might like to highlight key points as you go along, but do not cover the text in coloured ink – it will obscure meaning rather than enhance it.

Question

Turn the first heading into a question. So, for example, 'The role of organisation' becomes 'What is the role of organisation in improving memory?' Do the same for each subheading. You are beginning to elaborate on the material.

Self-recitation

Try to remember all of the key points from the section you have read. It often helps to recite this aloud even if you feel a bit silly! Check back with the text to make sure that you are recalling correctly.

Test

Test yourself on the whole chapter shortly after you have completed it. It is important to test yourself again at intervals to make sure that you have continued to remember it. Do not leave it until one frantic session the night before the exams!

Quick test questions

1 Which of the following are components of Atkinson and Shiffrin's multi-store model of memory?

- [ ] Sensory memory
- [ ] Phonological loop
- [ ] Long-term memory
- [ ] Short-term memory
- [ ] Central executive

2 Which of the following statements describe short-term memory?

- [ ] Limited capacity
- [ ] Loses information through decay
- [ ] Unlimited duration
- [ ] Prefers acoustic coding
- [ ] Transfers information to long-term memory through rehearsal

3 What does digit span measure?

- [ ] The capacity of long-term memory
- [ ] The duration of short-term memory
- [ ] Encoding in sensory memory
- [ ] The capacity of short-term memory
- [ ] Encoding in short-term memory

4 Which of the following are not components of the working memory model?

- [ ] Visual cache
- [ ] Central executive
- [ ] Sensory memory
- [ ] Long-term memory
- [ ] Articulatory loop

5 What is meant by a dual task technique?

- [ ] Participants are asked to recall a list of either short words or long words
- [ ] Participants are asked to recall a string of digits
- [ ] Participants are asked to do two different tasks simultaneously
- [ ] Participants are asked to recall a list of words after rehearsal has been prevented
- [ ] Participants are asked to recall information from many years ago

6 Which one of the following statements about KF is not true?

- [ ] He could learn new information and transfer it into long-term memory
- [ ] He could recall information stored in long-term memory
- [ ] He had a normal digit span
- [ ] His case study can offer support for the multi-store model of memory
- [ ] His case study can offer support for the working memory model

7 Which of the following is not a technique used in the cognitive interview?

- [ ] Cognitive reinstatement
- [ ] Recall in reverse order
- [ ] Report everything
- [ ] Ask misleading questions
- [ ] Recall from changed perspective

8 Which of the following mnemonic techniques are not based on visual imagery?

- [ ] Peg-word system
- [ ] Method of loci
- [ ] Keyword method
- [ ] Rhyming
- [ ] Taking the first letter from each word to be recalled and forming them into a sentence, e.g. 'Richard of York gave battle in vain'.

Exam-style questions

There are different kinds of exam questions that require you to use material differently. Marks available can range from 1 to 12. You must read each question carefully, follow the requirements, and write enough to access the marks available.

Knowledge questions

1 Here are some important terms from the memory topic. Explain what is meant by each of these:

Encoding; Capacity; Duration; Cognitive interview

2 Describe the working memory model. *(6 marks)*

> **AQA** **Examiner's tip**
>
> For 6 marks, you will need a detailed description of the model including the names of the different components of the model, their characteristics (e.g. capacity, duration and encoding) and their processes (e.g. attention, rehearsal). A well-labelled, accurate diagram could get you full marks. You do not need to evaluate the model in this kind of question and will get no marks for evaluation.

3 Outline how **one** research study has investigated the effect of age on the accuracy of eyewitness testimony. *(4 marks)*

> **AQA** **Examiner's tip**
>
> Choose just one study – you will not get marks for describing more than one. This question requires an outline of the methods and procedures so do not get bogged down in describing the findings of the study – include just enough for the examiners to identify the study you have chosen.

4 Cognitive interviews have been developed to improve witness recall. Identify and explain two techniques used in the cognitive interview.
(3 + 3 marks)
May 2009

> **AQA** **Examiner's tip**
>
> You only need to outline two of the techniques so do not waste time naming and describing all four. You need to name each of the two techniques (identify) for 1 mark and then explain what the technique involves for the other 2 marks.

5 Outline **one or more** strategies for memory improvement.
(4 marks)

> **AQA** **Examiner's tip**
>
> There is a breadth/depth trade-off here. You can describe one strategy in detail or more than one in slightly less detail.

Apply it

Remember to look at the number of marks allocated to decide how much depth and detail you need in your answer. Try writing 2-mark definitions for each of the terms in the first question. Now try to develop your answers into 3-mark definitions.

Application questions

1 The multi-store model has been criticised in many ways. The following observation illustrates a possible criticism.

Some students read through their revision notes lots of times before an examination, but still find it difficult to remember the information. However, the same students can remember the information in a celebrity magazine, even though they read it only once.

Explain why this observation can be used as a criticism of the multi-store model of memory. *(4 marks)*

January 2009

2 A psychologist showed participants a film of a fair-haired boy in a blue jumper stealing some sweets in a shop. The psychologist then asked them some questions about what they had seen. Half the participants were given a misleading question to see if it affected the accuracy of their recall. Give an example of a misleading question the psychologist could have asked in this study. *(2 marks)*

3 A researcher found that participants could successfully carry out a verbal and visual task at the same time but were not able to do two verbal tasks at the same time. How does the working memory model explain this finding? *(5 marks)*

> **AQA** Examiner's tip
>
> For application questions, remember to look for clues in the scenario. It may help if you underline these on the exam paper. You will not gain full marks if you do not relate your answer back to the scenario, and the underlining might help you to do this.

Methodological questions

1 How have psychologists investigated the capacity of short-term memory? *(4 marks)*

2 Describe **one** way in which psychologists have investigated the duration of short-term memory. In your answer, you should include details of stimulus materials used, what people were asked to do and how duration was measured. *(4 marks)*

June 2010

3 Outline **one** strength and **one** weakness of the working memory model. *(2 + 2 marks)*

> **AQA** Examiner's tip
>
> In this kind of question, the focus is on the procedure of the investigation and not on the findings.

Essay-style questions

1 Outline and evaluate the multi-store model of memory. *(12 marks)*

2 Outline and evaluate the working memory model. *(12 marks)*

3 Outline and evaluate research into the effects of anxiety on the accuracy of eyewitness testimony. *(12 marks)*

May 2009

4 Outline and evaluate the use of the cognitive interview. *(12 marks)*

Sample answers

Explain why it might be better to carry out research into eyewitness testimony in the real world, rather than in a laboratory.

(3 marks)

June 2010

If you do EWT research in a laboratory, it will be very artificial. Participants know they are going to be tested on what they see in a film and will be paying attention. In real life, when something like a robbery or a car crash happens, people are not expecting it and might not be paying attention. They are also likely to be more emotional or anxious in real life. This means that laboratory research will not show what people are like in real life and so is not as valid as real-world research.

The candidate is clearly referring to EWT research again and making a good point about what happens in the laboratory

The candidate has now made a clear contrast to what happens in a real-world situation

The candidate has started well by referring to EWT in the opening sentence – this means that they are focusing on this particular kind of research as required by the question and not writing a more general answer about laboratory versus real-world research

Another good point that differentiates real-world situations from laboratory set-ups

The candidate has offered a meaningful conclusion by explaining the advantage of real-world research in terms of validity

AQA Examiner's comments

This answer is relevant and well focused. It refers specifically to EWT instead of making general points about laboratory research lacking ecological validity. It is a good, full answer from the top band.

Outline and evaluate the multi-store model of memory.

(12 marks)

First sentence is not strictly necessary but, if you have time, it shows that you understand it is an early model

This is quite an important characteristic of the model

It is important to include this reference to processes as well as to the capacity, encoding and duration

There is sufficient detail on processes and structure for STM

The multi-store model was first proposed by Atkinson and Shiffrin in 1968. It consists of three separate stores each with its own characteristics. Memory flows through the stores in a series of stages but always in the same order. Information first goes into the sensory memory which holds things for a very brief period of time, has a very small capacity but can deal with information in all modalities (e.g. sight, hearing, smell, etc.). Information passes on to the short-term store if it is paid attention. If not, it fades from sensory memory and is completely lost. The short-term store has a capacity of about seven items and can hold information for up to about 30 seconds. If information is not rehearsed, it is lost. STM prefers to code acoustically. If information is rehearsed enough, it will pass into long-term memory. LTM can hold a limitless amount of information for up to a lifetime. LTM prefers to code semantically.

Succinct sentence showing the structure of the model and the fact that the stores all operate slightly differently

Succinct account of the features of sensory memory – if you can use the technical language appropriately, e.g. 'modalities', you do not need to explain them in brackets

There is sufficient detail on processes and structure for LTM

Outline and evaluate the multi-store model of memory.

(12 marks)

This is a good paragraph where lots of studies have been mentioned without going into unnecessary procedural detail

One strength of the model is that there is a lot of research evidence supporting the idea that the stores have different capacities, durations and encoding styles. For example, Miller showed that the capacity of STM is limited to about seven items while Baddeley showed that coding is usually acoustic in STM and semantic in LTM. The Brown-Peterson technique has been used to show the brief duration of STM and also the importance of the rehearsal process in holding information. Such studies have been replicated many times so provide reliable evidence.

Good to start a new paragraph for a new point

There is also evidence from clinical case studies such as Clive Wearing and HM to show that STM and LTM work in a different way. However, KF can be used both to support and undermine the model. He had a faulty STM and an intact LTM supporting the model. However, he could transfer items to LTM even though his STM was not working properly, showing that the fixed sequence through the model might not be right.

This is a good point

Good to use a phrase like this

This is linked to the fact that evidence supporting the model can be interpreted differently to support the working memory model.

The model is too simple and does not account for the fact that we can remember certain things better than others.

Two valid points, although neither is well explained

Remember that there are equal marks for AO1 and AO2 in this kind of question. Do not spend too much time on one or the other.

For full AO1 marks, you need to write about the structure and the processes of the model to show the examiner that you have real understanding. Try to use technical language (e.g. 'modalities', 'acoustic/semantic coding') – provided you use it appropriately, it will help you to write clearly and succinctly.

In this question you could draw diagram. If it is really well labelled and shows structure and processes, it could get you full AO1 marks.

The annotated sample answer is shown on the opposite page.

AQA Examiner's comments

This answer would achieve marks in the top band. The description of the model is accurate, detailed and shows sound knowledge and understanding. The evaluation of the model is balanced with points both for and against the model. Material has been used effectively to provide informed commentary.

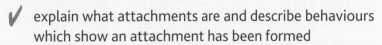
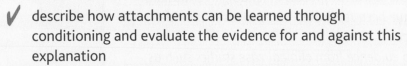

2 Developmental psychology

Attachment

Explanations of attachment

You need to know how to

✔ explain what attachments are and describe behaviours which show an attachment has been formed

✔ describe how attachments can be learned through conditioning and evaluate the evidence for and against this explanation

✔ explain Bowlby's theory of attachment and evaluate the evidence for and against it.

Babies demonstrate attachment behaviours from around six or seven months of age. You can tell that a baby has developed an attachment by two kinds of behaviour:

■ separation anxiety – distress when separated from the attachment figure

■ stranger distress – fear of strangers.

The learning explanation of attachment

■ As babies cannot feed themselves, they rely on other people to meet their biological needs for food.

■ Attachments are based upon feeding.

■ The baby associates the person who feeds them (usually the mother) with the pleasurable sensations of being fed and relief from hunger (classical conditioning).

■ The mother becomes a positive reinforcer (operant conditioning) as she provides rewards for the baby.

■ Attachments may also be learned via observation and modelling (social learning theory).

■ Parents act as role models for children, teaching them how to give and receive affection.

> This is a common-sense explanation of attachment, which was automatically assumed to be true for many years. However, it is contradicted by some studies of young animals and babies, which show that attachments are not simply based on feeding.

AQA **Examiner's tip**

Practise writing a 6-mark summary of the learning explanation of attachment. This could also be the topic of a 12-mark question.

Study	Method	What was found
Schaffer and Emerson (1964)	Observational study of 60 Glasgow babies	Around 4 in 10 babies formed their first attachment to someone who did not feed them but who played with them.
Harlow and Harlow (1958)	Gave baby monkeys, who had been separated from their natural mother, a soft cloth pretend 'mum' monkey and a wire 'mum' monkey, which fed them	The baby monkeys formed an attachment to the soft cloth 'mum', showing that comfort was more important than simply providing food.

These studies show that attachment requires more than simply feeding in order to develop as Bowlby suggested.

Evolutionary explanations of attachment: Bowlby's theory

Attachments are instinctive behaviours for both babies and parents that have evolved because they increase the likelihood of babies surviving.

Babies possess instincts (crying/smiling) to get others to look after them, and parents (especially mothers) possess instincts to protect and care for their babies.

Babies form one attachment which is more important than all others (monotropy).

This first attachment must be formed in the sensitive period before the child reaches the age of three.

The first attachment provides the baby with a model of how loveable they are and how trustworthy other people are. It also provides a prototype or internal working model (IWM) of how relationships work.

The attachment formed as a child affects later adult relationships (the continuity hypothesis).

AQA Examiner's tip

This is a likely topic for a 6- or 12-mark question. Practise writing a 6-mark summary of this theory and two paragraphs of evaluation. You could structure this into evidence for and against Bowlby's theory.

Evaluation of Bowlby's theory

Bowlby's theory has been extensively tested and many of his ideas have been accepted. It is widely acknowledged that mothers play an important role in their children's emotional as well as physical health. Other claims made by Bowlby have been refined as we have learned more about child development:

- IWMs and continuity: Hazan and Shaver's Love Quiz study (1987) found that attachments in childhood often predicted adult love relationships, supporting the idea of the IWM. However, attachment types can change depending on later experiences. Secure children who experience parental divorce/death may become insecure. Insecure children may develop 'earned security' from a later relationship.

- Monotropy: Bowlby's belief in the importance of mothering/parenting in later adjustment is widely accepted. However, Schaffer and Emerson (1964) suggest that multiple attachments rather than single attachments are common for most babies.

The sensitive period before the age of three is the best time for attachment to form. However, in circumstances of adoption or privation, attachments can be formed later than three years. Tizard and Hodges (1989) found that children adopted after the age of four still attached to their new parents.

Think about it

You can use Bowlby's explanation to evaluate the learning theory. Bowlby argues that attachment is an evolved mechanism. What evidence does he have for this claim?

What are the problems involved in studying young animals and assuming that findings also apply to human babies?

You can also evaluate Bowlby's theory by considering its impact on childcare policies and practices.

Types of attachment and the Strange Situation

You need to know how to

✔ explain the use of the Strange Situation in attachment research

✔ describe the behaviour of a securely attached child, an insecure-avoidant child and an insecure-resistant child.

Key study

The strange situation (Mary Ainsworth, 1970)

Sample: American toddlers aged 12–18 months and their mothers.

Method: Ainsworth used controlled observation in a laboratory 'playroom'. Eight episodes each lasting around three minutes were standardised. These involved the mother briefly leaving the baby alone, then returning and a stranger approaching the baby. The episodes were designed to measure separation anxiety and stranger distress.

Findings: Babies' behaviour fell into three broad types or patterns.

Attachment types

Type	A Avoidant	B Secure	C Resistant
Behaviour	Largely ignored the mother when she left and returned. Treated the stranger in a similar way.	Used their mother as a safe base to explore the playroom. Upset when mother left and pleased to see her when she returned. Wary of the stranger but accepted some comfort from them.	Upset when the mother left, but did not settle down when she came back. Alternated between being angry and clingy. Very worried about the stranger.

Conclusion: Ainsworth concluded that babies have different types of attachment with secure being most common. She argued that attachment type depended upon how quickly and sensitively mothers responded to their babies.

■ Secure babies had mothers who responded quickly and sensitively. They felt safe when the mother was there as she looked after them consistently.

■ Insecure babies had mothers who did not respond consistently. Some ignored their babies, and the babies learned not to expect very much (avoidant). Others responded inconsistently, so the baby became anxious and unsure how the mother would act (resistant/ ambivalent).

Think about it

A small number of the babies did not fall clearly into one of these three categories. This led other researchers to propose a fourth type: D, or Disorganised attachment. Not everyone agrees with Ainsworth's explanation of attachment types. Kagan believes that babies are born with a temperament, which makes some easy-going and others crabby and difficult – regardless of how their mother responds.

Cultural variations in attachment

> **You need to know how to**
>
> describe the method and findings of van IJzendoorn and Kroonenberg's meta-analysis of Strange Situations studies in different places
>
> link children's attachment behaviour to the ways in which they are brought up in different countries.

Babies are brought up in different places around the world and different qualities are encouraged in them. Ainsworth's Strange Situation study has been repeated (replicated) many times in different countries. These studies have shown that whilst secure attachments remain the most common across cultures, there are variations between different cultures and also within cultures.

van IJzendoorn and Kroonenberg (1988)

van IJzendoorn and Kroonenberg carried out a meta-analysis of 32 Strange Situation studies in different countries. The table below shows a summary of the percentage of babies showing each attachment type in four countries.

Attachment types shown by babies in different countries

Country	Avoidant (%)	Secure (%)	Resistant (%)
Great Britain	22	75	3
Israel	7	64	29
Japan	5	68	27
Germany	35	57	8

> **Think about it**
>
> Note the date of this study (1970). Social changes since the 1980s may influence the findings and affect children's attachment types. How might China's 'one child' policy have influenced how children are brought up and attachment patterns? How might the recent increase in working mums in Japan influence the kinds of attachment patterns shown?

How these findings reflect on the way children are brought up

In the UK, around 70 per cent of mothers work and children are put into nursery or with a childminder from a young age. In Germany, working mothers are rare (fewer than one in five mothers work) but young children are encouraged to be independent and self-reliant. These experiences may lead young children to show less anxiety about separation and be classed as avoidant.

In 1988, very few Japanese mothers worked and babies were rarely put in nursery or left with childminders. This explains why they showed violent protest at separation but did not settle down when the mother returned – they experienced few separations and were simply not used to them. This led to the increased number of resistant children.

In Israel, many children are brought up in communes called kibbutzim. In closed communities, they are unlikely to meet strangers, which explains why they show so much fear of strangers.

Disruption of attachment

You need to know how to

✔ explain what is meant by separation

✔ describe how children react to separation including the PDD model and separation anxiety

✔ understand the kinds of factors that influence how a child responds to separation.

Response to separation

Children can experience separations for different reasons. For example, a parent may go into hospital for a few days or a young child may be taken into care and placed with foster parents for a longer period of time. The PDD response to separation was identified by Robertson and Robertson (1969) in their study of John, a little boy who was put in a residential nursery while his mother had a baby. John showed *three stages of reaction* typical of young children.

Children's responses to separation

Stage 1: Protest	Stage 2: Despair	Stage 3: Detachment
Child may cling to the parent to prevent them leaving and cries and screams after they have gone.	Child sinks into a state of hopelessness or depression. They do not seem interested in anything.	The child appears to be better. They are no longer actively distressed but appear to have 'switched off' from people.

Long-term effects: separation anxiety

After the separation has ended, some children may continue to show effects. They may show increased separation anxiety about situations such as being left at nursery, which they previously coped with. They may become more clingy or may alternate between rejection of the parent and demanding their attention.

A number of factors affect how a child responds to separation. These include:

■ Age – children under about 18 months who have limited language skills find it more difficult to communicate with someone who does not know them well.

■ Who they are left with – if this is someone close who they are also attached to the effects will be less severe, especially if the person can interpret what the child wants.

■ Where they are left – if this is familiar (own home/grandparents' home) they may cope better than in a strange place.

■ Experience of previous separations – a child who has had previous good separations may cope better.

Apply it

A potential 'scenario' question could ask you how you could help a young child cope with separation. Make two lists, one showing the features of a good separation and the other showing a bad separation and use the two lists to devise strategies to help – what to do and what to avoid.

Think about it

These factors help us to understand why John's experience was so bad. Left with strange people in a strange place, unable to talk he must have felt frightened and bewildered.

Failure to form attachment

You need to know how to

 explain what is meant by privation and institutionalisation

 describe and evaluate research studies into the effects of privation and institutionalisation on children

 understand the factors that influence how well children recover from difficult early childhood experiences.

Privation

Most studies of privation consist of naturally occurring case studies of children who have been brought up in unusual circumstances and have experienced physical neglect and abuse as well as lack of attachment.

There are also studies of children who have been raised in institutions and experienced emotional privation (lack of attachment) but have not experienced physical privation (see Tizard and Hodges, page 26).

Privation case studies

	Koluchova (1972)	Skuse (1984)
Early life	Twin boys suffered extreme privation from 18 months to 7 years. They were locked in an unheated cellar, beaten and starved. They had no human company except each other.	Two girls experienced privation from birth until the ages of 2½ and 3½. Their mother had learning difficulties and kept them tied to the bed with dog leads. They were prevented from talking.
Problems	At age 7, they were unable to talk, terrified of adults and had severe health problems.	When found, they had no speech and very few social skills. They also did not know how to play.
Recovery	Following extensive treatment/ rehabilitation, the boys were placed in a permanent foster home. They developed normal language skills and attended mainstream schools.	Louise developed normal language skills and started school. Mary showed severe problems and was moved to a special school for autistic children.
Discussion points	Suggests that young children can sometimes recover from difficult circumstances if they receive good aftercare. It is hard to know what happened to the children during the first years of their lives. Each set of circumstances is different so we should not generalise from case studies. It is also difficult to know whether Mary suffered from some form of developmental delay or whether this was caused by neglect.	

AQA Examiner's tip

You may be asked to show your understanding of the strengths and weaknesses of case studies using a scenario question. It will help if you think of one of these example case studies when writing your answer. It is very hard to establish exactly what happened to the children in these studies and there are many gaps.

AQA Examiner's tip

Look back at the section on case studies. What strengths and weaknesses of case study evidence apply here?

Ethical issues

Case studies require sensitivity from the researcher to the children involved and their foster/adoptive parents. Both may feel under pressure to take part in research.

Institutional care

Some children are raised in institutions such as children's homes due to inadequate parental care or circumstances such as civil war. This is known as institutionalisation. Tizard and Hodges, and also Rutter, have studied the development of children who have spent time in institutions.

Key study

Tizard and Hodges (1984/89)

Sample: 65 children brought up in a children's home until at least age four.

Method: In this natural experiment, 65 children were raised in a home where the physical care was good, but staff were discouraged from forming attachments to children. By the time the children were two, they had on average 24 carers. At age four, 25 were restored to their birth parents, 33 were adopted and the remaining 7 remained in care. Some of the children were followed up at ages 8 and 16.

Findings:
Results of Tizard and Hodges' study

	Number showing a close attachment at age 8	Number showing a close attachment at age 16
Adopted children	20/21	17/21
Restored children	6/13	5/9

Both restored and adopted children struggled with relationships with peers and they were less likely to have a best friend.

Conclusion and implications: Children can form attachments outside the sensitive period of the first three years, contradicting Bowlby's claim of a sensitive period for attachment. However, they may struggle with relationships with people who do not put in extra effort. There may have been differences between the children, which led to some being adopted and others staying in the home, which could also affect the outcome of the study.

Can children recover from privation and institutionalisation?

Studies show that many children develop rapidly when adopted and form strong attachments. The degree of recovery depends on a number of factors:

- Length of time spent in the institution: Rutter *et al.*'s 2007 study of Romanian children found that those who were adopted after six months were more likely to show disinhibited attachment patterns than children adopted at an earlier age.
- Quality of emotional and physical care at the institution: those that allow children to form attachments to staff generally do better (Dontas *et al.*, 1985).
- The quality of care after leaving the institution: children generally do best when placed with a family who can give them lots of care and attention (Tizard and Hodges, 1989).

Attachment in everyday life

The effects of day care on social development

> ### You need to know how to
>
> explain the impact of day care on social development
>
> describe and evaluate research studies which have shown the impact of day care on children, including positive and negative effects.

Day care is care given when parents are at work, usually at nursery or by a childminder.

Social development refers to a child's ability to get on with other children, make friends, cooperate and share.

Types of day care

Nursery based	Family based
In a state or private nursery, there are lots of structured activities, play-workers and children to play with.	The child is looked after in the home by a nanny, childminder or relatives.
Children receive less adult attention than in a family setting and may become frustrated or aggressive when tired.	They are likely to get more adult attention and may develop language skills more rapidly.
They have lots of opportunities to make friends, learn to cooperate and share.	There are fewer children to play with and less opportunities to develop social skills and make friends.

> ### Apply it
>
> Make a list of the advantages and disadvantages of these two types of day care. Which do you think would be best for an only child and why? What about a very shy child?

The effects of day care

Peer relations

What they did	What they found	Discussion points
Andersson (1992) Studied social and cognitive progress of children attending Swedish day care.	Children who attended day care (DC) were able to get on better with other children, were more sociable and outgoing.	Need to be cautious in generalising findings from one place to another. Day care in Sweden is well funded and high quality. But findings are supported by other studies.
Schindler et al. (1998) Studied 57 children attending DC in the US. Observed over two-week period. Measured amount of time spent playing alone, alongside or co-operatively with other children.	Positive correlation between amount of time spent in DC and amount of time spent playing co-operatively with other children.	This is a correlational study so need to be cautious about claiming that DC causes more co-operative play. Co-operative play generally increases as children get older and more able to talk – this is a confounding variable. Other studies (e.g. DiLalla, 1988) found a negative correlation between amount of time spent in DC and pro-social play.
Campbell et al. (2000) Compared children in Sweden who attended DC between 18 months and 3½ years with home-raised children, following them until age 15.	Children who spend short days in nursery are more socially competent than home-raised children. Social competence stays around the same level from 3½ to 15 years.	Study showed that quality of DC has an effect as well as time spent in day care. Children were assessed before they started DC providing a baseline to compare their social abilities. Lengthy follow up period shows possible long term effects of early DC experiences.

Aggression

What they did	What they found	Discussion points
Campbell et al. (2000) (as above)	Children under 3½ years who spend long days in nursery have more negative interactions (squabbles) with other children and are less socially competent.	Small children spending long days in day care become tired and frustrated, leading to more negative interactions with other children.
Belsky (2006) Analysed data from a longitudinal study of 1000 American children followed from birth.	DC children showed higher levels of problem behaviours than non-DC children, including aggression towards peers and disobedience towards teachers and other adults.	American DC is lower quality and less well funded than DC in Sweden. Finding is supported by Maccoby and Lewis (2003) who also found that more hours in DC correlated with more conflict with teachers. One interpretation is that children who attend DC become more confident and assertive.
The National Institute of Child Health and Development (2003) Examined behaviour of a large sample of children aged 4½ years. Researchers collected reports about children's behaviour from parents, teachers and carers.	The more time a child spent in DC, the greater amounts of problem behaviours, including disobedience and aggression.	Used an extremely large sample so likely to be reliable. Study was in the US where DC is less well funded. Use of reports from parents and teachers provides well rounded data about children's behaviour.

Evaluation

- Both quality and quantity of DC affect the outcome for children.

- It is hard to draw conclusion from studies of DC as children attend for different lengths of time and start at different ages. They also have different personalities, e.g. a shy child may struggle more than an outgoing, confident child.

- The effects of DC also depend on the home environment. A child from a disadvantaged home may receive greater benefit than a child from a home with lots of advantages

Implications for day-care practices

You need to know how to

✔ explain how research into attachment has influenced how day care is organised and run.

You should be able to explain how research into attachment generally and Bowlby's theory specifically has influenced how day care is organised and run.

Implications of research into day care

Findings from research	Applications to policy or practice
Bowlby's theory states that children need a secure attachment with an adult who they can use as a safe base to explore their environment.	Many nurseries employ a key-worker system (Goldschmied and Jackson 1994). Each key worker is the named attachment figure for a small number of children. The key worker provides a safe base so the child can play and return to them when they need a cuddle. The childminder should form an attachment with the children in their care.
Children should be able to rely on their attachment figure in times of stress or when they are frightened.	The key worker/childminder needs to be available to the child at stressful times such as dropping off and collection as studies show these to be difficult times for young children.
Children can have multiple attachments with a range of different adults (Schaffer and Emerson, 1964).	Nurseries and childminders operate with a low child-to-adult ratio and follow strict rules about how many children can be looked after by one adult.

Good-quality care at nurseries requires:

- enough staff for children to receive individual attention

- staff who are well paid and trained so that staff turnover (staff leaving and new staff starting) is minimised – children need continuity and consistency at nursery

- small-sized groups so children are not overwhelmed by strangers

- a mixed age group so that pro-social behaviours can be copied from older children.

Think about it

These factors help to explain *why* day-care studies produce such different results. Good day care may lead to helpful, socially skilled children. Poor day care may lead to frustrated, stressed and insecure infants.

Quick test questions

1 Which two of these are characteristics of attachment behaviour?

- [ ] Separation anxiety
- [ ] Imprinting
- [ ] Stranger distress
- [ ] Detachment
- [ ] Protest

2 Which concept is not part of Bowlby's (evolutionary) explanation of attachment?

- [ ] Internal working model
- [ ] Safe base
- [ ] Monotropy
- [ ] Social learning
- [ ] Sensitive period

3 Which ideas are part of the learning explanation of attachment?

- [ ] Babies form attachments to people who feed them
- [ ] Attachments are rapidly formed through imprinting
- [ ] Skin-to-skin contact is important in forming attachments
- [ ] Children learn attachment behaviours through watching and copying their parents
- [ ] Attachments are based on rewards

4 Which three attachment types were found in the Strange Situation?

- [ ] Disinterested attachment
- [ ] Secure attachment
- [ ] Disinhibited attachment
- [ ] Insecure avoidant attachment
- [ ] Insecure resistant attachment

5 Which of these findings applied to van IJzendoorn and Kroonenberg's meta-analysis of cultural variations in attachment?

- [ ] There were more Chinese studies than from any other country
- [ ] There were more American studies than from any other country
- [ ] Secure attachments were the most common in all places
- [ ] German babies were more likely to be avoidant
- [ ] Japanese babies were more likely to be avoidant

6 Which of the following was the response to short-term separation in the Robertsons' study of John?

- [ ] Protest, detachment, disregard
- [ ] Protest, detachment, privation
- [ ] Protest, detachment, disinterest
- [ ] Privation, despair, detachment
- [ ] Protest, despair, detachment

7 What did Tizard and Hodges find in their study of privation?

- [ ] Restored children were most likely to have secure attachment at age eight
- [ ] Restored children had better relationships with siblings than adoptees
- [ ] Restored children were more llikely to have secure attachments at age 16
- [ ] All the institution children had problems with friends/peer relationships
- [ ] Adopted children were most likely to have secure attachment at age eight

8 Which of the following are characteristics of good-quality day care?

- [ ] Rapid turnover of staff
- [ ] Opportunities for children to form attachments with staff
- [ ] Plenty of adults so children receive lots of attention
- [ ] Large-sized groups so children have lots of friends to play with
- [ ] A mixed age group so children can copy pro-social behaviours from older children

Exam-style questions

There are different kinds of exam questions, which require you to use material differently. Marks available can range from 1 to 12. You must read each question carefully, follow the requirements, and write enough to access the marks available.

Knowledge questions

1   Here are some terms from the attachment topic. Explain what is meant by each of these:

Attachment; Secure attachment; Insecure-avoidant; Insecure-resistant; Privation; Institutionalisation; Day care; Social development

2   Outline Bowlby's explanation of attachment.   (6 marks)

3   Explain **two** differences in behaviour between a securely attached and an insecurely attached child.   (2 + 2 marks)

4   Outline **two** characteristics of high-quality day care.   (2 + 2 marks)

5   What have studies shown us about the effects of day care on aggression?   (6 marks)

6   What have studies shown us about the effects of day care on peer relations?   (6 marks)

Knowledge questions can appear in different formats with stimulus material to get you thinking. For example:

7   Many years ago, when young children went into hospital, parents were unable to stay the night with them and were encouraged to visit for a short length of time once a day. This experience was very stressful for young children and now parents are able to stay in hospital when young children are admitted. What has research shown about the effects on young children of short-term separations like going into hospital?   (4 marks)

Application questions

1   Research has suggested that institutionalisation can have negative effects on children. In the 1990s, many children were found living in poor-quality orphanages in Romania. Luca had lived in one of these orphanages from birth. When he was four years old, he was adopted and he left the orphanage to live in Canada. His development was then studied for a number of years. Outline possible negative effects of institutionalisation on Luca.   (4 marks)

2   Jane and Simon have recently become parents and their baby boy, Peter, is now eight months old. Jane is going back to work next month and Peter's grandparents live a long distance away and cannot look after him. Jane and Simon are considering what type of day care to choose for Peter. What would you tell them about the possible effects of nursery-based care on Peter's social development?   (4 marks)

Apply it

Remember to look at the number of marks allocated to decide how much depth and detail you need in your answer. Try writing 2-mark definitions for each of these terms. Now, develop your answer into a 3-mark definition.

AQA   Examiner's tip

For application questions, remember to look for the clues in the scenario. It may help to underline these.

---

3   Ali has just started working in a nursery that offers day care for young children from six months of age and above. She notices that the younger babies do not seem to mind when they are left at nursery, but many of the toddlers between one year and 18 months old become upset at drop-off time and seek comfort from their key worker. How might attachment theory explain the differences in response? What suggestions would be made by attachment theory to minimise stress to toddlers?   (*4 marks*)

Essay-style questions

1   Outline and evaluate the learning explanation of attachments.
                                                                (*10 marks*)

2   Outline and evaluate Bowlby's explanation of attachment.
                                                                (*12 marks*)

3   Outline and evaluate research into the effects of institutionalisation.   (*10 marks*)

4   Outline and evaluate research studies that have considered the impact of day care on aggression.   (*12 marks*)

Developmental psychology

Sample answers

Research has suggested that institutional care can have negative effects on children. In the 1990s, many children were found living in poor-quality orphanages in Romania. Luca had lived in one of these orphanages from birth. When he was four years old, he was adopted and he left the orphanage to live in Canada. His development was then studied for a number of years. Outline possible negative effects of institutional on Luca.

(4 marks)

Luca has been living in a poor-quality orphanage and has not been adopted until quite late in life (four years). He is unlikely to have had much adult attention and he might show some problems with cognitive skills like talking, reading and writing. If Luca did not have an attachment with an adult in the orphanage due to lack of staff, he will have suffered emotional privation. Luca might show signs of disinhibited attachment common in institutionalised children. He might be demanding from adults and very clingy and unable to share attention with siblings. He may struggle to make friends with peers.

The candidate makes a good start by referring to key elements of the scenario such as the quality of care and length of time Luca has been in the orphanage

The candidate has identified an important effect of institutionalisation and described the kinds of behaviours shown in disinhibited attachment

AQA — Examiner's comments

Clearly focused on effects. The answer covers cognitive and emotional effects and elaborates on both, explaining what type of problems Luca might have. The answer engaged with the scenario, picking up how long Luca's privation has gone on for. This answer would be in the top band.

The question is worth 6 marks and asks for studies, so the answer should include findings of two or more pieces of research in order to access higher mark

What have studies shown us about the effects of day care on peer relations? (6 marks)

Most studies have shown that day care has positive effects on peer relations. There have been more studies on nursery care than home-based care such as childminders. Children who go to nursery have lots of opportunity to meet other children and learn how to share, make friends and cooperate. Andersson (1992) found that Swedish children who attended DC were able to get on better with other children. Campbell (2000) found that Swedish children who spent short days in nursery were more socially competent than home-raised children. However, both of these studies were carried out in Sweden where day care is well funded and high quality and Belsky suggests that children become more aggressive when they attend day care in US studies. Schindler (1998) found that DC children were more helpful and pro-social than home-raised children, suggesting that good helpful behaviour is encouraged at nursery.

This sentence shows good understanding of the benefits of nursery based care

This is a good section – the findings of lots of studies are summarised without going into too much depth

AQA   Examiner's comments

Clearly focused on the question and describes the findings of a range of studies. Although not asked to evaluate, reasons are given for why studies may produce different findings. This material gives extra depth and detail to the description of research studies. This answer would achieve a mark in the top band.

3 Research methods

Methods and techniques

> **You need to know how to**
>
> describe and evaluate these research methods:
>
> experimental methods (laboratory, field and natural); studies using correlational analysis; observational techniques; self-report techniques (questionnaires and interviews); case studies.

The research methods section contains material that is used in the study of all the topics in Psychology. You may be asked questions in which you need to apply your knowledge of research methods and techniques to scenarios in questions for either of the units.

> **AQA** **Examiner's tip**
>
> When evaluating methods, you need to be aware of their strengths and weaknesses. These can be practical or ethical.

Experiments

Terminology

- **Independent** and **dependent variables** (**IV** and **DV**). The IV is the variable that the researcher manipulates and which is assumed to have a direct effect on the DV. The DV is the variable that is affected by changes in the IV.
- **Extraneous variables** (**EVs**) are any variables other than the IV that might affect the DV. It is important for the researcher to try to get rid of as many of these as possible. If they are left in, they could affect the DV and become confounding variables.

In an experiment, researchers want to see the effect of one thing (the independent variable) on another thing (the dependent variable). For example, they might want to investigate the effect of alcohol (IV) on short-term memory span (DV). The most basic way of doing this is to divide the IV into two levels: alcohol and no alcohol.

- In the experimental condition, participants are given a predetermined quantity of alcohol and then given an immediate digit span test.
- In the control condition, participants are given no alcohol, just the immediate digit span test.

In this experiment, the IV is whether or not the participants drink alcohol and the DV is their score on the immediate digit span test.

Comparing experiment types

	Laboratory	Field	Natural
What is it?	Researcher directly manipulates IV to see its effect on DV. Takes place in highly controlled conditions	Researcher directly manipulates IV to see its effect on DV. Takes place in natural setting	Researcher takes advantage of a naturally occurring event to see its effect on DV (NB: the IV is not directly manipulated).
Strengths	High level of control of IV and EVs Replicable Can infer cause and effect	Higher ecological validity (than in laboratory) Reduction in participant effects (demand characteristics) Can infer cause and effect	Useful where it would be impossible/unethical to manipulate the IV or undertake the investigation in a lab setting High levels of ecological validity
Weaknesses	Artificiality can lead to low validity. Strong chance of investigator and participant effects	Less control over EVs Less control over participant sample Difficult to replicate exactly Can be more time-consuming to set up and carry out	Lack of control of EVs – leads to low internal validity Less possible to infer cause and effect confidently Less control of participant sample Difficult to replicate or generalise as the natural event is usually a one-off
Ethical issues	It is sometimes impossible to gain fully informed consent because of potential demand characteristics.	Consent, deception and right to withdraw are all important issues as participants often do not realise they are in an experiment.	Consent, right to withdraw and confidentiality are all important issues.

Think about it

Remember that a laboratory is any setting where the conditions are highly controlled – the study does not have to take place in a traditional laboratory.

Correlational analysis

Positive correlation

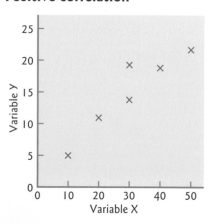

Negative correlation

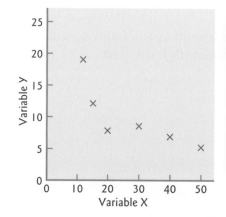

Summarising correlation

What is it?	Technique for analysing data by measuring the strength of the relationship between two variables. The analysis will show one of three things: ■ a positive correlation (as one variable increases, the other variable increases) ■ a negative correlation (as one variable increases, the other variable decreases) ■ no correlation.
Strengths	Can establish the strength of a relationship between two variables and measure it precisely Allows researchers to investigate things that could not be manipulated experimentally for ethical or practical reasons
Weaknesses	Cannot establish cause and effect Can only measure linear relationships (i.e. clear positive or negative correlations) – does not detect curvilinear relationships
Ethical issues	Consent, confidentiality and right to withdraw are issues as participants are often unaware their data is being used.

> **Think about it**
>
> A correlational analysis cannot detect a curvilinear relationship (or inverted U relationship). This is where there is a positive relationship only up to a certain point, after which it becomes negative. A good example is the relationship between arousal and performance. If you are bored or unmotivated, you are not likely to perform well. If you are stimulated, you can perform really well. If you become over-stimulated or exhausted, your performance starts to get worse.

Observational techniques

Before any scientific observational study takes place, the researcher has to decide on the particular behavioural categories or events to be investigated. See p41 for a summary of how this is done.

> **AQA** **Examiner's tip**
>
> Do not confuse a naturalistic observation with a naturalistic experiment.

Comparing naturalistic and controlled observation

	Naturalistic observation	Controlled observation
What is it?	Researcher observes participants in their own environment. No deliberate manipulation of variables	Researcher observes participants in a controlled environment. Often involves manipulation of variables, e.g. in Ainsworth's Strange Situation
Strengths	High ecological validity Participants usually behave more naturally. Useful preliminary research tool – can suggest hypotheses for further research	Higher level of control over EVs
Weaknesses	No control over EVs	Participants usually know they are being observed – might not behave naturally – lowers validity
Ethical issues	Privacy, confidentiality and consent are important issues.	Informed consent, confidentiality and right to withdraw are issues.

Self-report techniques

These include questionnaires and interviews where participants are asked directly about their feelings, beliefs and attitudes. These techniques rely on the participants' honesty. Sometimes what people say they will do is not what they would actually do in real life.

<table>
<tr><td>Think about it</td></tr>
<tr><td>Remember, a structured interview is very like a questionnaire except that it is delivered face to face. It is the unstructured interview that differs most from a questionnaire.</td></tr>
</table>

Terminology

- **Closed questions** require participants to answer yes/no or choose from fixed responses determined by the researcher (quantitative data).
- **Open questions** allow the participant to answer in their own words (qualitative data).
- **Structured interview**: all participants are asked the same questions in the same order. Can provide quantitative data.
- **Unstructured interview**: an informal, in-depth conversational exchange between interviewer and interviewee. Some general questions are usually thought about in advance, but the interview follows the interviewee's answers. Provides rich, qualitative data.

Comparing questionnaires and interviews

	Questionnaire	Interview
What is it?	A set of questions, used to collect data from a large sample of participants Can be given face to face, by post, phone or internet, or simply left in public places	Researcher asks participants questions directly face to face. Can be structured or unstructured
Strengths	Can reach a large sample of people relatively quickly and cheaply Can collect large amounts of data Time efficient as researcher does not have to be present Reduces investigator effects Data can be easily analysed (if quantitative) Replicable	**Structured** Data analysis straightforward Less risk of investigator effects Less training needed for interviewers Interviewer available to clarify any ambiguity **Unstructured** Researcher can follow up issues raised by interviewees. Interviewee can expand on answers so provide new insights. More informal – interviewer can be more sensitive when asking for personal information.
Weaknesses	Social desirability/lack of honesty – leads to low validity Postal surveys have low response rate – reduces representativeness of sample. Questions may be ambiguous (and researcher is not there to explain). Questions (if closed) limit the depth of the response. Questions (if open) can be difficult to analyse.	**Structured** Interviewer cannot follow up interesting answers. Formal situation may inhibit honest/full answers. **Unstructured** Interviewer effects Social desirability High level of training needed for interviewers Time-consuming and expensive Can be difficult to analyse qualitative data
Ethical issues	Privacy, protection from harm, confidentiality and informed consent.	Privacy, protection from harm, confidentiality, informed consent and right to withdraw.

Examiner's tip

You could be asked to give advantages of a using a questionnaire rather than an interview. If this happens you must explain the strength of a questionnaire compared to an interview in order to gain marks. In other words, you will not get credit for saying: 'Questionnaires are quick.' You need to write something like: 'Questionnaires take less time than interviews because the researcher does not have to be present when they are completed.'

Think about it

Some people are less honest when filling in a questionnaire than they would be in an interview and some are more honest. Can you think why this might be?

Case studies

	Case study
What is it?	An in-depth study of an individual or group of people
Strengths	Provides rich data
	High levels of ecological validity
	Can suggest new hypotheses for further research
	Can investigate topics that would be impractical/unethical to investigate experimentally
Weaknesses	Difficult to replicate
	Difficult to generalise results
	Possibility of researcher bias
Ethical issues	Informed consent, invasion of privacy, right to withdraw and confidentiality are all issues.

Think about it

Think back to the memory section and the case of Clive Wearing or of HM. Why have these case studies been useful in helping us to understand human memory and what are the problems involved in generalising from these findings?

Investigation design

You need to know how to

 be familiar with these features of investigation design:

aims; hypotheses; experimental design; design of naturalistic observations, questionnaire and interviews; IV, DV and EV; pilot studies; reliability and validity; awareness of the BPS Code of Ethics and how psychologists deal with ethical issues; demand characteristics and investigator effects; random opportunity and volunteer sampling.

Aims and hypotheses

Terminology

- An **aim** is a statement about the purpose of the investigation – what the researcher is trying to discover.
- A **hypothesis** is a precise, testable statement about the expected outcome of an investigation. In experiments, this is called the experimental hypothesis. In other types of investigation, for example correlations, it is called the alternative hypothesis.

Directional and non-directional hypotheses

The experimental/alternative hypothesis can be **directional**, which predicts the direction of the difference/correlation, e.g. 'participants will recall more short words than long words in a serial recall task' or 'there will be a positive correlation between reading speed and the number of digits recalled in an immediate digit span task'.

They can also be **non-directional**, which do not predict the direction of any difference/correlation, e.g. 'there will be a difference in the number of words recalled in a serial recall task depending on whether the words are short or long' or 'there will be a correlation between reading speed and the number of words recalled in an immediate digit span task'.

Experimental design

Once a researcher has decided on the hypothesis, they have to decide which design to choose.

What is it?	Strengths	Weaknesses
Repeated measures design Same participants in each condition	Holds individual differences constant so controls for them Needs fewer participants	Order effects (e.g. fatigue, learning, boredom) Increased chance of demand characteristics Cannot use same set of stimulus materials in both conditions
Independent groups design Different participants in each condition (randomly allocated to avoid any bias)	No order effects Reduced likelihood of demand characteristics Can use same set of stimulus material in both conditions	Individual differences can affect the result More participants required
Matched pairs design Participants matched on key participant variables, e.g. gender, age, social background, intelligence	No order effects Reduces effects of individual differences Can use same set of stimulus material in both conditions	Difficult to decide on criteria for matching Difficult to match exactly More participants required

Design of naturalistic observations

Terminology

- **Observer bias** describes the effect on results caused by the fact that an observer can have their own interpretation of a piece of behaviour that is different from others.

- **Inter-rater reliability** is the extent to which two observers agree in their rating of their same behaviour. It is usually measured by taking both sets of ratings and comparing them using correlational analysis.

- **Behavioural category** is a specific type of behaviour that is defined before the start of the study. It allows observers to focus on the precise kind of behaviour being investigated.

Think about it

Sometimes, there is no choice of design, e.g. if the IV is sex then an independent groups design must be chosen – males in one group and females in the other. Usually the choice is not that straightforward and there are pros and cons whichever design you choose.

Apply it

Imagine your hypothesis is, 'Participants who drink caffeine will recall more digits in an immediate digit span than participants who do not'. You could choose any of the three designs but each would have advantages and disadvantages. Write down the advantages and disadvantages for each of the three designs with regard to this hypothesis.

AQA Examiner's tip

Remember the difference between method and design.
If you are asked about the method used in a particular investigation, the answer will be something like 'lab experiment', 'case study', 'observation', etc.
If you are asked about the experimental design, you already know that the investigation must be an experiment – you will now have to decide what type of design has been used, i.e. repeated measures, independent groups or matched pairs.

What you need to consider when designing a naturalistic observation

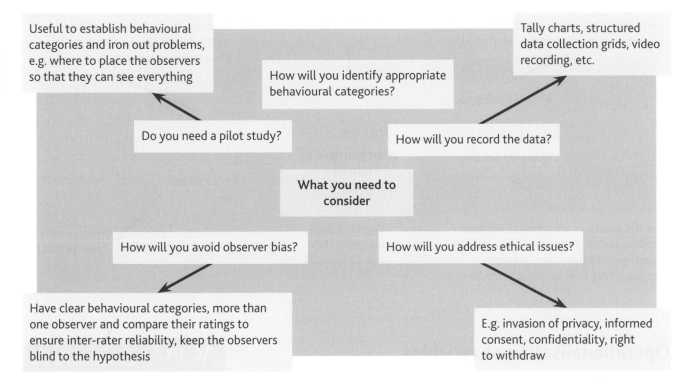

Useful to establish behavioural categories and iron out problems, e.g. where to place the observers so that they can see everything

How will you identify appropriate behavioural categories?

Tally charts, structured data collection grids, video recording, etc.

Do you need a pilot study?

How will you record the data?

What you need to consider

How will you avoid observer bias?

How will you address ethical issues?

Have clear behavioural categories, more than one observer and compare their ratings to ensure inter-rater reliability, keep the observers blind to the hypothesis

E.g. invasion of privacy, informed consent, confidentiality, right to withdraw

Design of questionnaires and interviews

Terminology

- **Response set** can be a problem with the design of questionnaires. It is when questions are set out in a such a way as to lead participants into a fixed mindset. There is a tendency for people to agree with test items as a habitual response. This can be avoided if about half of the items on a questionnaire are positive towards the topic and half are negative, so participants have to think about each item individually.

What you need to consider when designing a questionnaire

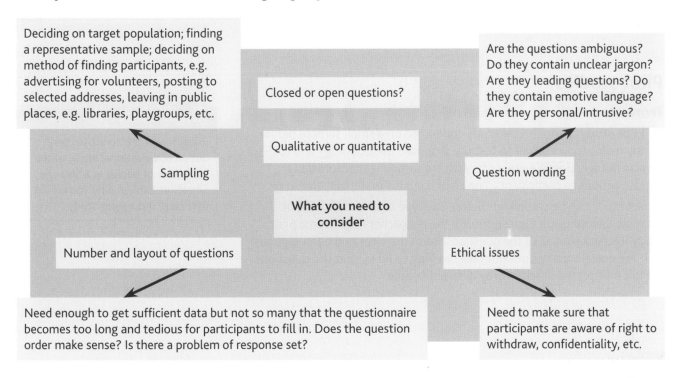

Deciding on target population; finding a representative sample; deciding on method of finding participants, e.g. advertising for volunteers, posting to selected addresses, leaving in public places, e.g. libraries, playgroups, etc.

Closed or open questions?

Are the questions ambiguous? Do they contain unclear jargon? Are they leading questions? Do they contain emotive language? Are they personal/intrusive?

Qualitative or quantitative

Sampling

Question wording

What you need to consider

Number and layout of questions

Ethical issues

Need enough to get sufficient data but not so many that the questionnaire becomes too long and tedious for participants to fill in. Does the question order make sense? Is there a problem of response set?

Need to make sure that participants are aware of right to withdraw, confidentiality, etc.

What you need to consider when designing an interview

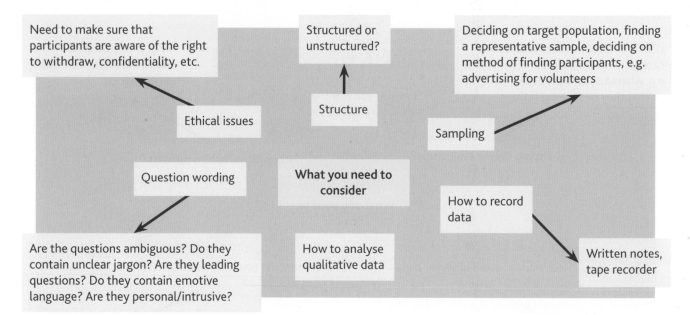

Need to make sure that participants are aware of the right to withdraw, confidentiality, etc.

Ethical issues

Structured or unstructured?

Structure

Deciding on target population, finding a representative sample, deciding on method of finding participants, e.g. advertising for volunteers

Sampling

Question wording

What you need to consider

How to record data

Are the questions ambiguous? Do they contain unclear jargon? Are they leading questions? Do they contain emotive language? Are they personal/intrusive?

How to analyse qualitative data

Written notes, tape recorder

Operationalisation of variables

Terminology

- **Operationalisation** is the process of precisely defining how a variable can be measured. This makes the study replicable.

Example: investigating the effect of age on the accuracy of eyewitness testimony

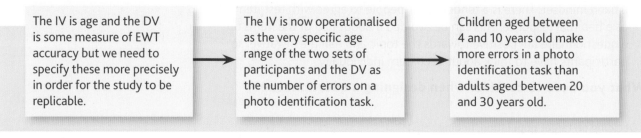

The IV is age and the DV is some measure of EWT accuracy but we need to specify these more precisely in order for the study to be replicable.

The IV is now operationalised as the very specific age range of the two sets of participants and the DV as the number of errors on a photo identification task.

Children aged between 4 and 10 years old make more errors in a photo identification task than adults aged between 20 and 30 years old.

Pilot studies

Terminology

- **Pilot study**: a small-scale study conducted on a small sample before the main study in order to test the proposed methodology and to iron out any possible problems with the sampling method, design, instructions to participants, choice of stimulus materials, and so on.

A pilot study can be carried out before any type of investigation. For example, before using a questionnaire the researcher might run a pilot study to check that all of the questions/items are clear and unambiguous, that the questionnaire does not take too long to fill in, that the questions are not interpreted differently by different people.

Control of extraneous variables

It is not always possible to remove every single EV, but it is important to eliminate as many EVs as possible.

Types of EV that researchers need to bear in mind when designing studies

Participant variables

Intelligence, age, gender, personality, etc.

Choosing an appropriate design – repeated measures design or matched-pairs avoids individual differences

In independent groups design, randomly assigning participants to conditions helps to avoid bias

Demand characteristics

Cues in the environment that help participants to work out what the research hypothesis is This can make them alter their behaviour artificially.

Single blind technique, i.e. making sure that the participants do not know what the hypothesis is and do not know which condition they are in (more difficult in repeated measures designs)

Experimenter effects

Characteristics of the investigator that might affect participant responses, e.g. age, gender, etc.

At an unconscious level, the investigator might behave in such a way as to influence the outcome of the study in favour of their own predictions.

Double-blind technique, i.e. neither the participants nor the investigator know the hypothesis or the condition the participants are in. This involves a research assistant carrying out the data collection for the main experimenter.

Situational variables

Temperature, time of day, lighting, stimulus material used in study, etc.

Standardisation, i.e. making sure conditions and materials are the same for all participants as much as possible.

Standardised instructions so everyone is doing the same thing.

Reliability and validity

Terminology

- **Reliability** refers to the consistency of results. If you carry out the same study again or measure something using the same tools again, you should get the same results.

Validity

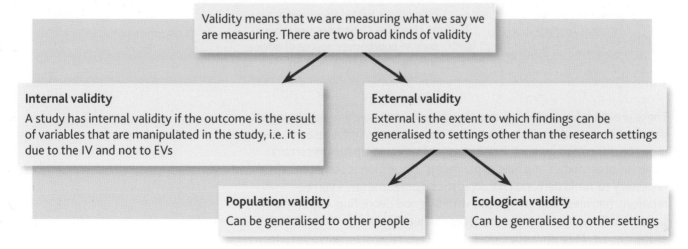

Validity means that we are measuring what we say we are measuring. There are two broad kinds of validity

Internal validity

A study has internal validity if the outcome is the result of variables that are manipulated in the study, i.e. it is due to the IV and not to EVs

External validity

External is the extent to which findings can be generalised to settings other than the research settings

Population validity

Can be generalised to other people

Ecological validity

Can be generalised to other settings

The British Psychological Society (BPS) Code of Ethics

The BPS is the professional organisation responsible for promoting ethical behaviour in the UK and it has developed a set of ethical principles designed to protect the public from harm and to maintain the integrity of British psychologists.

For the up-to-date version of the Code, see the BPS website (www.bps.org.uk).

You will not need to know every detail set out in the Code for the exam but you will need to be aware of some of the major ethical guidelines.

AQA Examiner's tip

Where deception has been deemed necessary and acceptable, debriefing is especially important but do not make the mistake of thinking that debriefing alone makes deception acceptable.

Ethical guideline categories

Consent – aims of research should be made clear to participants. Parental consent must be obtained for children under age of 16.

Deception – information should not be withheld and participants should not be misled.

Debriefing – participants should be given a full explanation after the study has been completed.

Confidentiality – participants have the right to confidentiality, i.e. their data must be kept anonymous. In rare cases where confidentiality cannot be assured, participants must be clearly informed of this before they agree to take part in the study.

Right to withdraw – participants have a right to withdraw from the study at any time even if they have been paid to take part. They can even withdraw at the end of a study and, in this case, any data collected from them has to be destroyed.

Ethical guidelines

Protection of participants – psychologists have a responsibility to protect their participants from physical and emotional harm. Participants should not be exposed to more risk than they would be in everyday life.

Observational research – protection from harm can be a particular issue for observational studies. Privacy is an important issue when consent has not been obtained – participants should not be observed in situations where they would not normally expect others to watch their behaviour.

Giving advice – if psychologists become aware of a possible physical or psychological problem in any of their participants or if the participants themselves ask for advice from the psychologist, the psychologist must proceed with caution. Psychologists should only offer advice within their own area of expertise. Otherwise they should seek an appropriate source of advice and refer the participants on.

Colleagues – research psychologists usually work alongside colleagues in research settings. Where psychologists suspect that a colleague might be following an unethical procedure, they should intervene and raise their concerns with the researcher concerned.

These are guidelines not laws, and there are instances where psychologists cannot adhere to them if they want to carry out meaningful research, e.g. it can be difficult to gain informed consent from participants in certain observational studies and field experiments. Deception is sometimes necessary to avoid demand characteristics. Sometimes this can be relatively harmless and easily dealt with by good debriefing, e.g. some of Loftus' EWT studies. Sometimes, deception leads to much more serious problems, e.g. Milgram's obedience study. Psychologists always have to weigh up the risks and benefits of any research they carry out. One of the main checks is the need for them to publish their work in reputable journals. Research reports are rigorously scrutinised and journal editors will not publish studies where ethical guidelines have been ignored unless there is a very good reason.

Ethical issues and ways in which psychologists deal with them

AQA / Examiner's tip

You might be given a scenario and asked to identify an ethical issue arising from it. Make sure that the issue is relevant to the scenario and that you can explain why it is an issue. You may also be asked how a researcher may deal with the issue, so make sure that you choose an issue for which you can provide a solution.

There are two main ways of dealing with ethical issues in psychological research:

■ Self-regulate using the BPS Code of Ethics
■ Use ethics committees.

Ethical issue	Why is it an issue?	Methods for dealing with it
Deception	Participants may be misled about the nature of the research. It prevents them from making an informed decision about taking part. It might make people distrustful of psychologists.	Debriefing Retrospective informed consent
Informed consent	If participants are not given all of the facts before agreeing to take part in a study, they may find themselves taking part against their wishes. It might make people distrustful of psychologists.	Prior general consent Presumptive consent For children, gaining consent of parents or those in loco parentis (e.g. headteacher)
Protection from harm	Participants have a right to be protected from any physical or emotional harm. The participants should leave the study in the same state as they entered it. Any harm could have long-lasting effects.	Reminding participants throughout of their right to withdraw Terminating any research which appears to be causing distress Debriefing Offering advice/support

Terminology

Types of consent:

■ **Prior general consent** involves obtaining a general agreement to participate in a study that involves deception at some time in the future. In later studies, where they participate, it is then assumed that they will not object to being deceived.

■ **Presumptive consent** involves taking a random sample of the population and introducing them to the research, including any deception involved. If they agree that they would still have given their consent to take part, it is assumed that other people in the general population would also agree.

■ **Retrospective consent**: once the true nature of the research has been revealed, participants are given the right to withdraw their data.

Selection of participants and sampling techniques

Terminology

■ **Target population**: a group of people the researcher is interested in studying.

Selection of participants

It is usually not possible to investigate a whole target population because it is too large, it would take too long, it would cost too much, and you do not have access to all members of that target population.

So, you need to choose a *sample* from that population. The sample should be *representative* of the target population so that findings from the study can be *generalised* to the target population. If the sample is not representative it is a *biased* sample, and the validity of the study is called into question (it is said to lack *population validity*).

Relative strengths of three sampling techniques

	Random	Opportunity	Volunteer
What is it?	Sample in which every member of the target population has an equal chance of being picked	Sample that consists of people readily available to the researcher, e.g. a class of students, children attending a particular nursery	Sample where participants self-select, e.g. they respond to an advertisement asking for volunteers
How is it obtained?	Every member of the target population is identified and then a random sampling technique is applied.	The researcher approaches people who happen to be available and asks them if they would be willing to take place in the research.	The researcher advertises for volunteers on posters or in magazines/newspapers.
Issues	Most likely to be a representative sample of the target population (although cannot guarantee it) Difficult to obtain because must have access to every member of the target population – usually only possible where the target population is quite small If anyone drops out or refuses to take part, the sample becomes less random.	High chance that the sample will not be very representative of the target population Sometimes people feel obliged to take part even if they do not really want to, e.g. students where the researcher is their teacher. Most popular technique because it is so convenient	A certain type of person tends to volunteer and this means that there is a high chance that the sample will not be representative. Useful way of finding participants for highly specific types of research, e.g. on adults whose mothers have died when they were children.

AQA   Examiner's tip

Practise writing definitions of the sampling methods. Make sure that you really explain what it is, e.g. 'A random sample is one where you pick the names randomly' does not explain what is meant by random sampling.
A good check is to ask yourself if someone would be able to understand how to obtain a random sample by reading your definition.

Data analysis and presentation

> **You need to know how to**
>
> analyse, present and interpret data, including:
>
> graphs, scattergrams and tables; measures of central tendency and dispersion; correlations (positive, negative and coefficients); qualitative and quantitative data; processes involved in content analysis.

Presentation and interpretation of quantitative data

Graphs are a way to display data in a meaningful way. It is useful to know about four different types of graph: bar charts, histograms, frequency polygons and scattergrams.

- All four types of graphs are drawn with two axes (sides).
- The vertical axis is called the *y*-axis.
- The horizontal axis is called the *x*-axis.

Terminology

- **Nominal data** are data placed in categories, for example the number of people with blue eyes, brown eyes, etc. Each category is mutually exclusive, which means that a participant can only appear in one category.
- **Ordinal data** are data that can be put into rank order, e.g. exam marks, ratings of aggressiveness, birth order in a family, etc.
- **Interval data** are data that are measured in terms of equal intervals, e.g. minutes, centimetres, degrees, items in a memory test, etc.

Bar charts

- A bar chart is used for nominal data.
- It consists of a set of vertical bars with a space between each of them.
- Each bar represents a different category (non-continuous data).
- The bars can be placed in any order along the *x*-axis.
- The categories are shown on the *x*-axis.
- The frequency of each category is shown on the *y*-axis.

Bar chart showing types of attachment in a group of 18-month-old babies

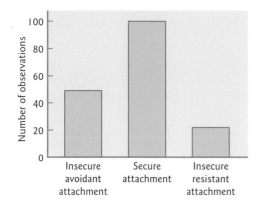

> **Apply it**
>
> A researcher wants to know which toys are the most popular in a playgroup. He asks the 80 children who attend the playgroup to say which their favourite toy is.
>
> Of the responses 20 say the sandpit, 5 say the play tent, 14 say the trains, 12 say the play kitchen, 10 say the ball, 9 say the dressing-up clothes and 10 say the building bricks.
>
> Try plotting this information on a bar chart. Give it a suitable title and label the axes appropriately.

Histograms

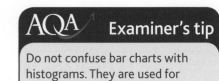

- A histogram consists of a series of vertical bars of equal width.
- The bars are continuous so there is no space between them.
- It is used for ordinal or interval data.
- The units of measurement are shown on the *x*-axis.
- Single values can be used on the *x*-axis, or data can be grouped.
- Frequency is represented by the area of each bar. In cases where the class widths are all equal, you can use the value that they go up to on the *y*-axis as equivalent to their area.

Histogram to show the number of digits recalled in an immediate digit span test (non-grouped data)

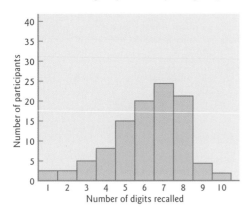

- Histograms can be used to show data grouped together into class intervals.

For example, participants are asked to do a cognitive task as quickly as possible and they are timed.

Here are the raw scores:

Participant 1	Participant 2	Participant 3	Participant 4	Participant 5
1 m 30 s	1 m 25 s	2 m 3 s	58 s	3 m 29 s
Participant 6	**Participant 7**	**Participant 8**	**Participant 9**	**Participant 10**
2 m 18 s	1 m 10 s	1 m 1 s	1 m 48 s	4 m 1 s
Participant 11	**Participant 12**	**Participant 13**	**Participant 14**	**Participant 15**
2 m 13 s	3 m 33 s	1 m 19 s	2 m 14 s	3 m 2 s

Each score is different so it would not be useful to plot the individual scores on a histogram. In this case we could group the data as so: 0–59 sec, 1 min–1 min 59 sec, 2 min–2 min 59 sec, 3 min–3 min 59 sec, 4 min–4 min 59 sec.

Histogram taken to complete a cognitive task

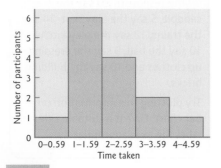

Frequency polygon

- This can be used as an alternative to the histogram.
- It is particularly useful when you need to show two sets of data on the same graph.

Frequency polygon to show the number of short and long words recalled in a serial recall test

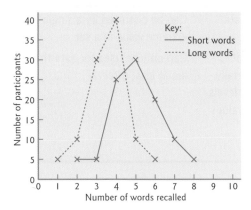

Scattergram (scattergraph)

- This is used for showing the relationship between two variables, that is for showing correlations.
- Data from one variable are shown on the *y*-axis and data from the other variable are shown on the *x*-axis.

A scattergram shows whether there is a trend towards a positive or a negative correlation (refer to p36). The closer the points on the graph are to a straight line, the stronger the correlation.

Analysis and interpretation of quantitative data

Measures of central tendency

Measures of central tendency are averages, that is single values that are calculated to represent a set of numbers by providing the most typical (central) value. The three measures of central tendency are:

- the mean (the arithmetic average – add all the scores and then divide the total by the number of scores)
- the median (rank the scores in order and then take the middle value)
- the mode (the most frequently occurring value).

In a normal distribution, the mean, median and mode all coincide. However, for most sets of data, they will provide different values.

For example, in the following set of scores:

3 4 5 5 5 5 6 6 8 8 10 10 10 32 33

the mean = 10, the median = 6 and the mode = 5.

Therefore, it is important to choose the most appropriate measure of central tendency that best reflects the data.

AQA Examiner's tip

You may be more familiar with the term 'averages', but the correct term is 'measures of central tendency'. You could be asked a question about this in the exam, e.g. 'Suggest an appropriate measure of central tendency for the data in this study.'

AQA Examiner's tip

Psychologists usually treat data such as scores on a memory test, reading test, intelligence test, etc. as interval data even though they are, strictly speaking, not measured on a true interval scale.

Central tendency measures

	Mode	Median	Mean
Advantages	Easy to calculate Only measure of central tendency for nominal data Unaffected by extreme scores	Can be used on ordinal or interval data Unaffected by extreme scores	Most sensitive measure taking all the scores into account
Disadvantages	Tells us nothing about other scores in the set and may not be typical (central) Limited usefulness if there is more than one modal score in a set Not useful for small sets of scores	Not much use for small data sets Can be unrepresentative of the data if scores are generally clustered at high and low levels or if there are only a few values in a set	Can be distorted by a single extreme value in a set Can only be used for data that are at least interval

Measures of dispersion

These show how the scores in a set are spread out. This is important because it tells us whether the scores are similar to one another or whether they vary hugely.

The two measures that you need to know for the exam are:

- range – the difference between the highest and lowest score in the set of data
- standard deviation (SD) – the average amount that each score differs from the mean.

AQA Examiner's tip

You may be asked to identify and explain the most appropriate measure of central tendency or dispersion in a novel situation.

Measures of dispersion

	Range	Standard deviation (SD)
Advantages	Quick and easy to calculate	Can be easily distorted by extreme values
Disadvantages	Takes account of all the scores	More difficult to calculate compared to the range Should only be calculated on data measured on an interval scale

Analysis and interpretation of correlational data

See also correlational analysis (p36) and the section on scattergrams on (p49).

Terminology

A correlation is a relationship between variables. Correlations can be positive or negative.

- **Positive correlation**: as values on one variable increase, so do values on the other variable.
- **Negative correlation**: as values on one variable increase, values on the other variable decrease.

- **Correlation coefficient**: a statistic that measures the strength of the relationship (correlation) between two variables. The scale of measurement ranges between +1 (perfect positive correlation) and −1 (perfect negative correlation). The numerical value indicates the strength of the relationship. The closer the numerical value is to +1, the stronger the positive correlation. The closer the value is to −1, the stronger the negative correlation. A numerical value of 0 means that there is absolutely no correlation between the two variables.

Example

Imagine that you have shown in a correlational analysis that children who score highly on reading tests also score highly on spelling tests. In other words, there is a positive correlation between reading and spelling ability. What could explain this?

There are three possible explanations:

- Children who read well are good at spelling because reading exposes them to the look of many different words.
- Children who spell well find reading easy because they do not have to puzzle over every word.
- Some other factor accounts for both spelling and reading expertise, for example a shared cognitive mechanism, encouragement from parents at home.

In order to investigate the causal connection, you would have to set up an experimental study.

Presentation of qualitative data

Terminology

- **Quantitative data** comes in numerical form, for example. distances expressed in metres, scores on a memory test, yes/no answers on a questionnaire.
- **Qualitative data** cannot be expressed in numbers and are obtained from, for example interviews or observations.
- **Content analysis** is a systematic research technique for analysing non-numerical data, e.g. material contained in interviews, documents, children's comics, TV programmes, newspapers, adverts, etc., making it quantitative.

Qualitative data collected from, for example, an interview can be very rich and detailed. They can take the form of what was actually said in the interview (a transcript of the actual words used); observations of body language, facial expressions, etc. during the interview; self-report from the interviewees about their feelings during the interview, etc.

Such material can provide valuable insights for a psychologist, but:

- It is very difficult to analyse the data and make sense of them for other people to understand.
- It is open to bias where the researcher makes selections and interpretations that fit their own theoretical standpoint or that are particularly relevant to their own research.

In order to make the data more accessible, some researchers choose to use the method of content analysis.

AQA Examiner's tip

You need to know what a correlation coefficient is and how to interpret it. However, for the exam, you do not need to know how to calculate it.

AQA Examiner's tip

Remember: the major disadvantage of correlational analysis is that you cannot infer cause and effect. The correlation only shows that there is a relationship between two variables. It does not show that one variable causes the other.

Apply it

Imagine you are writing a questionnaire about people's attitudes to smoking. Think of one suitable question which would provide quantitative data and one suitable question which would provide qualitative data.

Processes involved in content analysis

1 Decide what material to sample. For example, if the area of interest is personal adverts, the researcher would probably want to sample a range of different publications (newspapers or journals that reflect different political leanings, target readership, price, locality). If the researcher is interested in looking at the content of TV adverts, they might want to have a narrow focus (e.g. just those adverts that are on during children's programmes) or to have a wider focus, looking at different commercial channels at various times of the day/night.

2 Decide what type of themes and categories of response might emerge from these materials. In the traditional model of content analysis, themes are decided before the material is looked at. This can be done by using pilot studies or simply through the familiarity of the researcher with the type of materials being investigated. However, some researchers only decide on the themes after the sample materials have been gathered.

3 Create a coding system based on the predetermined themes.

4 The researcher usually collects a large number of examples of their chosen sample materials.

5 Coders are given the sample materials to read and asked to categorise items found in the materials according to the coding units.

6 Examples of coding units are:

- words – analyse for status-related words in personal adverts
- themes – analyse for examples of helping behaviour in children's comics
- character – analyse for gender stereotypical behaviour in TV adverts.

Content analysis is an effective way of presenting qualitative data in a way that is easy to understand. It can have high validity because it is usually gathered in natural settings.

However, the interpretation of the data can be subjective. In identifying the coding units, researchers can be inconsistent or impose their own meaning systems on the data. For this reason, the technique is often unreliable. One way to try to improve reliability is to have multiple coders who negotiate the coding units together. Correlational techniques (see p36) are often used to check the reliability of coders.

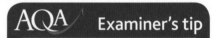

AQA Examiner's tip

You need to be able to describe how to do a content analysis and to apply this knowledge in the context of memory or attachment.

Quick test questions

'A study in which the investigator manipulates the independent variable in a natural setting.'

1 Which of the following corresponds to the above description?

- ☐ Laboratory experiment
- ☐ Field experiment
- ☐ Correlational analysis
- ☐ Questionnaire
- ☐ Case study

2 Which of the following hypotheses are directional?

- ☐ People will remember more short words than long words in a serial recall task.
- ☐ There will be a correlation between hours spent in day care and aggressive play behaviour.
- ☐ There will be a difference in accuracy on a visual task between people who have had caffeine and people who have not.
- ☐ There will be a negative correlation between scores on a stress test and scores on a health test.
- ☐ Clients with stress will show greater improvement after treatment with cognitive behavioural therapy than with drugs.

3 Which of the following are examples of open questions?

- ☐ Does your child attend day care?
- ☐ How many hours per week does your child attend day care?
- ☐ Tick the type of day care your child attends – nursery/playgroup/childminder
- ☐ Why do you choose to send your child to day care?
- ☐ What does your child enjoy most about day care?

4 The variable measured by the investigator to see if it has been affected by the IV is the:

- ☐ extraneous variable
- ☐ dependent variable
- ☐ confounding variable
- ☐ independent variable
- ☐ co-variable

5 Which of the following are examples of random sampling?

- ☐ A teacher asks her class of students to be participants in an experiment.
- ☐ A teacher has access to a list of all 400 children in a school. He selects every twentieth name on the list to obtain a sample of 20 children.
- ☐ A teacher has access to a list of all 600 children in a school. He puts each name on a separate slip of paper, jumbles them up in a hat and picks out 45 names.
- ☐ A teacher puts up a notice in the entrance hall of her school asking for children to sign up if they are interested in taking part in a memory experiment.
- ☐ A teacher has access to a list of all 500 children in her school. She gives them all a number and then consults a random number table to select 50 numbers.

6 Which of the following statements apply to a bar chart?

- ☐ It is used to show correlations.
- ☐ It is used for nominal data.
- ☐ It can be used for interval data.
- ☐ It consists of a set of vertical bars.
- ☐ The bars are continuous so there is no space between them.

7 Which of the following are measures of central tendency?

- ☐ Mode
- ☐ Median
- ☐ Range
- ☐ Standard deviation
- ☐ Mean

8 Which of the following are examples of qualitative data?

- ☐ A set of children's drawings
- ☐ Scores on a memory test
- ☐ Rank order of children in a class in terms of their birth dates
- ☐ A transcript of an interview
- ☐ TV adverts shown during children's programmes

Exam-style questions

Knowledge questions

Research methods questions are embedded in Section A (Cognitive Psychology) and Section B (Developmental Psychology) of PSYA1. Sometimes, the question will simply require knowledge with no application. For example, you might be asked to define some key research terms.

AQA — Examiner's tip

Usually such questions are for 2 marks, but sometimes they are worth only 1 mark and other times they are worth 3 marks. Remember to look at the number of marks allocated and decide how much depth and detail you need in your answers.

Try writing 2-mark definitions for the following terms:

Term	Examiner's tip
A field experiment	Make sure that you define both parts. Do not just say: 'It is an experiment carried out in natural setting.' Show that you understand what is meant by an 'experiment' as well.
A directional hypothesis	You need to define 'hypothesis' as well as 'directional'. Do not just say 'It is a hypothesis that predicts results in a particular direction.'
A pilot study	You need to mention both the scale and timing of the study.
Reliability	Do not confuse this with validity.
Random sampling	Do not say: 'This is a way of choosing participants at random.' This does not tell the examiner that you know what 'random' means in this context.
Demand characteristics	Do not confuse the characteristics with participants' reaction to them. Demand characteristics are the conscious or unconscious cues that reveal an investigator's expectations of his participants' behaviour.
A scattergram	You need to explain that this is a kind of graph that shows correlations. You can sketch one if you find it easier than writing an explanation.

Remember to read the question carefully and answer the question that is set. For example, there is a difference between the following two questions:

1   What is meant by the term 'pilot study'?   (*2 marks*)

2   Why do researchers sometimes carry out a pilot study?   (*2 marks*)

Similarly, there is a difference between:

3   What is meant by the term 'opportunity sampling'?   (*2 marks*)

4   How might a researcher obtain an opportunity sample?   (*2 marks*)

Contextualised questions

Try writing an appropriate answer to each of these questions.

Research methods questions are usually related to a stem or scenario and you will be required to apply your knowledge of research methods to this novel situation. For example:

> *HM was a young man who had undergone brain surgery to alleviate his epilepsy. Unfortunately, this left him with a severely impaired memory. Psychologists have studied this young man extensively in order to find out exactly how his impaired memory works.*

5 The scenario above is an example of a case study. Outline one strength and one limitation of this research method. *(2 + 2 marks)*

Try answering Question 5 and then have a go at substituting other types of method. For example:

> *A researcher staged a robbery in a shopping mall. In one condition, robbers, played by actors, had masks on and, in the other condition, the robbers wore no masks.*

6 The scenario above is an example of a field experiment. Outline one strength and one limitation of this research method. *(2 + 2 marks)*

> *A researcher recorded the amount of time that children spent in day care from birth to five years. She then asked their infant school teacher to rate each child for levels of aggression when they first started school. The researcher then compared the length of time in day care with the ratings of aggression. She found that the longer the children spent in day care, the higher the level of aggression.*

7 The scenario above is an example of a correlational analysis. Outline one strength and one limitation of this research method.

(2 + 2 marks)

In some research methods questions, you will find several questions all related to the same stem. For example:

> *A psychology teacher wanted to see if people are able to recall more short words than long words in an immediate serial recall test. Participants were asked to take part in two conditions. In Condition One, they were briefly shown five one-syllable words on a computer screen. They were then asked to write down the five words in the correct order. They had to do this 20 times with a new list of five short words each time. The psychology teacher then calculated the mean score of correct answers for each participant. In Condition Two, the same participants were briefly shown five multi-syllable words on a computer screen. They were then asked to write down the five words in the correct order. They had to do this 20 times with a new list of five long words each time. The psychology teacher then calculated the mean score of correct answers for each participant.*
>
> *Half the participants did Condition One first and half the participants did Condition Two first.*

When all the trials were completed, the following results were found:

Number of words recalled correctly

	Short words	Long words
Mean	4.5	1.9

AQA Examiner's tip

You won't be asked this many questions about one stem – this is just an example of the range of questions you might get.

1 What is the independent variable (IV) in this study? (*2 marks*)

AQA Examiner's tip

Do not just write: 'The words.' You need to make it clear that the IV is whether or not the words to be recalled are short or long.

2 What is the dependent variable (DV) in this study? (*2 marks*)

AQA Examiner's tip

It is not sufficient to say 'The score' or 'The number of words'. The DV is the number of short and long words correctly recalled in serial order.

3 What experimental design was used in this study? (*1 mark*)

AQA Examiner's tip

Make sure you remember that 'design' does not mean the same as 'method'. The method is experimental but the design is repeated measures.

4 Explain one strength of this experimental design in the context of this study. (*2 marks*)

AQA Examiner's tip

Make your answer relevant to this particular study. In this case, the major strength of a repeated measures design is that it tests the same people, so it controls for individual differences in memory ability.

5 Write a suitable directional hypothesis for this study. (*2 marks*)

AQA Examiner's tip

You must write a directional hypothesis. A non-directional hypothesis will get no marks. The question also says 'suitable', so look at the stem and at the results table, which should tell you which way the results are expected to go.

6 The psychology teacher used students in his class as participants for this study. Identify this type of sampling method. Explain your answer. (*3 marks*)

AQA Examiner's tip

The expected answer here is 'opportunity sampling', which is when a researcher uses a group of people who happen to be readily available. Either random or volunteer sampling could be acceptable here provided you explain it appropriately, e.g. you could assume that the researcher is a university teacher with over 100 students. He has not got time to test them all, but as he has access to a list of all their names he can choose a random sample of 20.

7   Explain why the researcher asked the participants to carry out the recall test 20 times for short words and 20 times for long words.

(2 marks)

AQA   Examiner's tip

What would happen if each participant only had one short-word list and one long-word list? It might be that they misunderstood what they had to do, coughed just as the list was presented, felt very nervous, and so on. This would mean that their score on the list would not truly represent their ability on this task. By giving the participant 20 trials (or goes) and taking their mean score, it is more likely that inconsistencies will be evened out.

8   The researcher calculated the mean scores. Name one other measure of central tendency and explain how to calculate it.

(2 marks)

AQA   Examiner's tip

In this question, you are not asked to apply your answer to the stem. You can name either the median or the mode, but you must make sure that you match the name to the correct method of calculation.

9   Explain why half the participants did Condition One first and half did Condition Two first.   *(2 marks)*

AQA   Examiner's tip

This is an example of counterbalancing. You do not need to know this term but it is helpful if you do – it is used in repeated measures designs to stop order effects. In other words, if all of the participants did Condition One first and Condition Two second, they might have performed better on Condition Two because they had practice. Alternatively, they might have been worse on Condition Two because they were becoming tired or bored. Either way, their performance was being influenced by an extraneous variable instead of by the IV.

10   The researcher carried out a pilot study before the main experiment. Explain why he might have decided to do this.   *(3 marks)*

AQA   Examiner's tip

You are not being asked to *define* a pilot study here. You have to think why it might be useful in this particular study. Things to consider here are the number of words that should be included in the lists, the types of words that are suitable for the short and long lists, the number of trials needed and the time of exposure of the list on the computer screen.

4   Biological psychology

Stress as a bodily response

The body's response to stress

> **You need to know how to**
>
> ✔ describe the hypothalamic-pituitary-adrenal stress system (or HPA axis)
>
> ✔ describe the sympathomedullary stress pathway (SAM).

What is stress?

Although we all experience what we call stress, scientists need a definition they can all work with. This definition is based on how we perceive the world around us (the source of stress), and how we perceive our coping abilities. This means that our sense of being stressed depends very much on cognitive processes.

When an imbalance or discrepancy exists between perceived demands and perceived coping resources, then a state of *stress* exists.

When the demands on us seem greater than our abilities to cope, we become stressed. This has immediate physiological effects – the body's response to stress. There are two main pathways. They both target the adrenal glands, which lie just above the kidneys. Each adrenal gland consists of two components – the adrenal cortex and the adrenal medulla – that release specific hormones when the pathways are activated.

> **AQA** **Examiner's tip**
>
> Make sure that you can identify the four or five key components of each pathway in the correct sequence. You must also be able to outline the functions of each component within the system.

Hypothalamic-pituitary-adrenal (HPA) axis

Activation of the HPA axis is slower as the activating hormone ACTH has to travel in the bloodstream from the pituitary gland to the adrenal cortex. Corticosteroids, such as cortisol, are released from the adrenal cortex. They mobilise stored energy reserves, providing increased blood levels of glucose and fatty acids that can be burned up in physical activity.

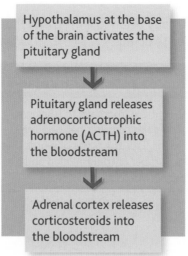

Hypothalamus at the base of the brain activates the pituitary gland

↓

Pituitary gland releases adrenocorticotrophic hormone (ACTH) into the bloodstream

↓

Adrenal cortex releases corticosteroids into the bloodstream

> **Think about it**
>
> Physiology can be difficult. It may help you to understand the body's response to stress if you think about your own reactions to sudden stress or excitement. Can you sense your heart rate increasing and feel a general sense of arousal? Try to explain this using the HPA and SAM pathways.

Sympathomedullary (SAM) pathway

Activation of the SAM pathway by stress results in impulses travelling rapidly from the brainstem centres via neural pathways (nerves) to the adrenal medulla. Adrenaline and noradrenaline released into the bloodstream travel around the body. They increase heart rate and blood pressure, speeding up the supply of oxygen to the muscles so it can be used in physical activity.

The main function of HPA and SAM activation is to provide the physiological resources for physical activity. They are systems that evolved when responses to stress would usually involve fighting or fleeing.

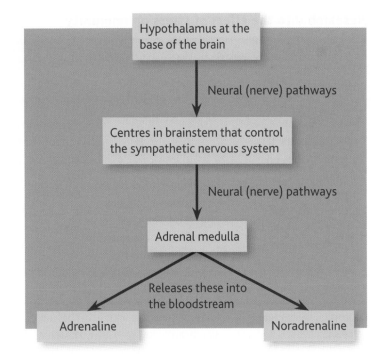

Stress-related illness and the immune system

You need to know how to

✔ describe the structure and functions of the immune system

✔ describe and evaluate research studies into the relationship between stress, immune function, and illness

✔ draw conclusions about the relationship between stress-related illness and the immune system.

Besides their actions in mobilising energy reserves, corticosteroids released as part of the stress response also dampen down our immune system. This system is the body's defence against infection and disease, so potentially we are more vulnerable to illness when our immune system is weakened by stress. The immune system has two main subdivisions as shown below.

Types of immunity

Natural immunity – this system is based on white blood cells in the bloodstream. These attack and ingest (absorb) any invading pathogens such as viruses and bacteria. Natural immunity is relatively fast-acting (minutes or hours).

Specific immunity – this division of the immune system is more sophisticated. The cells that make it up, called lymphocytes, have the ability to recognise invading pathogens and produce specific antibodies to destroy them. The specific immunity response is slower than natural immunity as its cells have to recognise the virus or bacteria and then produce the antibodies.

AQA Examiner's tip

The immune system is extremely complicated, so try to be clear on a few basic principles. Understand the two components: natural immunity (a rapid response system) and the slower specific immunity.

Apply it

Can you outline methods used by psychologists to investigate stress and the immune system?

Research into the effect of stress on immunity

What they did	What they found	Discussion points
Cohen et al. (1993) Some 394 participants rated their stress level and also completed questionnaires on stressful events experienced in the previous year and depression. These three things combined to give a 'stress index' score.	On exposure to the common cold virus, 82 per cent became infected. Of these, after seven days, the most stressed were most likely to get a full-blown cold as they could not fight it off. A higher 'stress index' correlated significantly with the chances of developing a cold.	Immune function was not measured directly. Correlational studies cannot confirm cause and effect. The high-stress group may have been more vulnerable to colds due to factors such as drinking, smoking and poor diet.
Kiecolt-Glaser et al. (1984) Seventy-five medical students preparing for their final examinations completed questionnaires on negative life events and social isolation. Immune function was measured via activity of natural killer cells before ('low stress') and during the exams ('high stress').	Immune function was significantly lower in the high-stress condition and the reduction was greater in students reporting high levels of social isolation. They concluded that examination stress significantly weakens immune function.	They used a direct measure of immune function, but did not investigate any illness outcomes. The study is not generalisable as it only used medical students as the sample. Follow-up studies by Kiecolt-Glaser with other groups showed similar outcomes, which strengthens the conclusions.

Think about it

The Cohen and Kiecolt-Glaser studies use very different methods to investigate stress and the immune system. Can you think of any advantage of using different methods in stress research? These two studies can be criticised, but in science it is the overall pattern of findings that allows us to reach conclusions. If 10 studies show similar findings, then our general conclusions will be more valid.

Segerstrom and Miller (2004) reviewed many studies of stress and the immune system. They concluded that:

- Short-term stressors lead to increased natural immunity, that is, the non-specific immunity system responds rapidly to immediate stressors.
- Long-term or chronic stressors lead to a weakening of both natural and specific immunity, a condition known as global immunosuppression. This overall weakening of our immune system leaves people vulnerable to illness.

Research has shown that stress weakens the immune system and can lead to illness. However, it is important to remember that many people are exposed to high levels of stress but only a few develop stress-related illnesses. Explaining these individual differences is an important part of stress research.

Apply it

Studies in this area often use questionnaires to assess levels of stress in people's lives. Can you state two advantages and two disadvantages of using questionnaires in stress research?

Stress in everyday life

Life changes and daily hassles

You need to know how to

✔ describe and evaluate research using Holmes and Rahe's SRRS (social readjustment rating scale)

✔ evaluate the role of life changes and daily hassles as sources of stress-related illness.

Life events

■ The first stage in stress research is to identify sources of stress in people's lives, and then to develop methods of measuring them.

■ Life changes are major life events such as marriage, serious illness or death of a partner.

Holmes and Rahe (1967) asked 394 people to assess the personal impact or stress value of 43 life events. Death of a spouse (partner) was rated as having most impact and was given a value of 100. Then other events were scaled in relation to death of a spouse.

■ Adding up the values for events experienced in the previous year gives a life change score for an individual.

Examples from the Holmes and Rahe social readjustment rating scale (SRRS or life event scale)

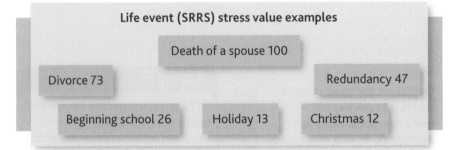

Life event (SRRS) stress value examples

Death of a spouse 100

Divorce 73   Redundancy 47

Beginning school 26   Holiday 13   Christmas 12

Weaknesses of SRRS

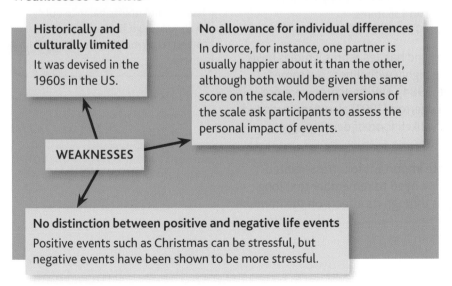

Historically and culturally limited
It was devised in the 1960s in the US.

No allowance for individual differences
In divorce, for instance, one partner is usually happier about it than the other, although both would be given the same score on the scale. Modern versions of the scale ask participants to assess the personal impact of events.

WEAKNESSES

No distinction between positive and negative life events
Positive events such as Christmas can be stressful, but negative events have been shown to be more stressful.

Research into the effect of stress on illness

Holmes and Rahe proposed that life event stress could lead to illness. For instance, scoring over 300 on their scale was associated with a 50 per cent increase in the chance of stress-related illness.

What they did	What they found	Discussion points
Rahe *et al.* (1970) Some 2,500 male US Navy personnel completed the SRRS (life event scale) for the previous six months. They were then monitored for seven months, and all stress-related illnesses were recorded.	There was a significant positive correlation of 0.118 between life event stress scores and illness scores. They concluded that life event stress can lead to illness.	Although significant, 0.118 is a very low correlation, suggesting only a weak relationship between life stress and illness. Correlational studies cannot confirm cause and effect (see Cohen *et al.* (1993) discussion point). Low generalisability due to specific sample

Daily hassles

Many studies have used the SRRS. Some fail to find a relationship between life event stress and illness, and correlations are usually low.

Lazarus and his research group (Kanner *et al.*, 1981) felt that a key problem was that life events are not common, and that the main source of stress for most people was everyday problems, so they devised the hassles and uplifts scales.

Hassles and uplifts

Hassles are daily problems: commuting to college or work, problems with friends, family strife, homework issues, etc. The original scale had 117 items.

Uplifts are the small positive things that can happen every day: good marks for homework, making new friends, receiving compliments on your appearance. The original scale had 135 items.

In direct comparisons of life event scores and hassles scores, studies have found that hassles scores correlate more highly with illness outcomes (De Longis *et al.*, 1982; Stone and Neale, 1984). Uplifts scores were not related to health outcomes. Evans and Edgerton (1991) also demonstrated that daily hassles scores could predict the likelihood of developing a clinical cold.

This suggests that everyday stress is more important for stress-related illness than major life events. However, we need to remember that long-term stress is also associated with illness through its effects on the immune system (see pp58–60).

Workplace stress

You need to know how to

 explain how workload and control affect workplace stress

 describe and evaluate research into sources of workplace stress.

Sources of workplace stress

Physical environment
High noise levels and increases in temperature can lead to frustration and stress. Office layout can also be a factor.

Home–work interface
With increasing numbers of women in the workplace, families are having to cope with increasing tensions between work and home.

Sources of workplace stress

Workload and control
It seems obvious that extreme workloads can be stressful, but research has shown that having too little to do can also cause stress. Workload interacts with control, also known as decision latitude. High levels of personal control reduce workplace stress, while low levels of control are one of the main sources of stress at work. Karasek (1979) put forward a model of the relationship between workload (demand) and control (decision latitude). The most stressful jobs combined high demand with low levels of control, and the least stressful had low levels of demand combined with high levels of control.

Workplace stress study

What they did	What they found	Discussion points
Marmot *et al.* (1997) Followed up over 7,000 UK civil servants over five years. All started free from heart problems. A range of workplace stressors were factored in, along with lifestyle factors such as drinking, smoking and obesity.	Workers in the lowest grades had 1.5 times the rate of heart disease compared to those in the higher grades. The most significant factor was the degree of personal control (decision latitude) over workload.	Questionnaires were used and self-serving bias can be a problem, e.g. under-reporting drinking and smoking. This would emphasise the effects of workplace stressors over lifestyle factors. This was a sample of office workers only, so although a mix of sexes were used, it is not very generalisable.

Think about it

One important application of research into workplace stress is that employers can use the results to change organisational structures and processes to reduce stress levels. Can you think of a realistic example of this?

Marmot *et al.'s* conclusions are supported by a very different study. Johansson *et al.* (1978) found that key factors leading to high stress levels in a Swedish sawmill were low levels of control, high levels of responsibility and machine-paced work.

Personality factors and stress

You need to know how to

✔ describe personality factors, including Type A and Type B behaviour, and hardiness, and how they relate to susceptibility to stress

✔ outline and evaluate research studies on the relationship between personality factors and stress.

Type A and B behaviour patterns

Life stress and workplace stress can lead to illness, but some people are more vulnerable than others. Not everyone exposed to high levels of stress becomes ill. One area that has been investigated is the role of personality, in particular the Type A behaviour pattern (TAB).

Friedman and Rosenman first described the TAB in the 1960s, and proposed that it was linked to an increased chance of developing stress-related heart disease. This was because Type A people had high levels of physiological activity (activation of the stress pathways, see pp58–9) and were easily frustrated and stressed.

The Type A behaviour pattern

Time pressured – always working to deadlines, often multitasking, unhappy doing nothing

Competitive – high achieving, playing to win whether at work or playing games and sports

Hostile – impatient with co-workers, easily angered

The Type B pattern is the opposite: relaxed, easy-going, not competitive or easily angered.

Think about it

How do we measure Type A behaviour? Questionnaires are a popular method, or alternatively a structured interview is used. A set series of questions is asked, and the trained interviewer notes the answers and also behavioural signs of Type A behaviour such as finger tapping and speed of talking.

Type A and B study

What they did	What they found	Discussion points
Rosenman *et al.* (1976) Categorised 3,454 American men as Type A or Type B using structured interviews. They were followed up for 8.5 years. Lifestyle factors such as smoking, drinking and obesity were controlled for.	Across the whole sample there were 257 heart attacks, with 69 per cent occurring in the Type A group. The researchers concluded that the TAB pattern was an important risk factor for stress-related heart disease.	The study has high ecological validity, but it is possible that some lifestyle variables related to heart disease might not have been controlled for.

There are significant findings, but many studies find little or no relationship between TAB pattern and stress. This has led researchers to analyse TAB in more detail. From looking at the results of many studies, Miller *et al.* (1996) found that the component of hostility is more strongly linked to heart disease than any other aspect of TAB.

Hardiness

The hardy personality is seen to be resistant to the negative effects of stress. It has three components that can be measured using questionnaires:

- **Control**: the sense that you are in control of events in your own life.
- **Commitment**: a strong sense of involvement and purpose in life.
- **Challenge**: life events are seen as opportunities rather than as sources of stress.

Personality factors clearly influence responses to stress. In particular, negative emotions such as anger and hostility seem to be linked to increased risk of heart disease. However, many studies are correlations, so cause and effect cannot be identified. It may be that, for instance, anger and hostility are also associated with risky lifestyles, such as increased drinking and smoking.

Hardiness

What they did	What they found	Discussion points
Kobasa *et al.* (1985) Used questionnaires to assess control, commitment and challenge. Also assessed levels of physical exercise and social support.	High scores on characteristics of hardiness, physical exercise and social support were all associated with lower levels of stress-related illness. 'Hardiness' had the greatest protective effect.	Studied male executives in white-collar jobs, so ecological validity is low and generalising is difficult. Design was correlational, so cause and effect cannot be assumed.
Beasley *et al.* (2003) Study on the effects of life stress on students.	Students who scored higher on hardiness showed lower levels of psychological distress.	Supports and generalises the findings of Kobasa (1979) and Kobasa *et al.* (1985) on protective effects of hardiness against stress-induced illness. But this was also a correlational study.

The concept of hardiness has been adopted as a way of developing resistance to stress. 'Hardiness training' is a form of cognitive behavioural therapy that aims to improve an individual's levels of control, commitment and challenge. However critics (Funk, 1992) point out that it is difficult to find a precise definition of the three components and so it is difficult to measure them reliably. Also, the research studies tend to be correlational, so the supposed protective effects of hardiness may in fact be due to some variable that has not been controlled or measured.

Think about it

Why was it important for the researchers in Rosenman *et al.*'s study on Type A behaviour and heart disease to try to control for lifestyle factors such as smoking and obesity?

Apply it

Look at the features of Type A behaviour and of the hardy personality. Can you identify any of these features in yourself and your friends? Most people will be a mix of the two personalities.

Psychological and biological methods of stress management

You need to know how to

✔ describe stress inoculation therapy (SIT) as a method of stress management

✔ describe the use of drugs as a method of stress management

✔ evaluate methods of stress management.

In everyday life each of us will try to manage stress using, for example, emotion- or problem-focused strategies. If stress becomes too great, we may then seek help from more systematic psychological or physiological methods of stress management.

SIT: a psychological method of stress management

Cognitive behavioural therapy (CBT) targets both cognitive processes, such as how we perceive the situation, and also tries to alter behaviour in positive ways. One popular form of CBT used in stress management is Meichenbaum's stress inoculation therapy (SIT). This consists of three stages.

AQA Examiner's tip

The marks available for each question on the examination paper are a clear guide as to how much you should write. For 3 marks you might be able to briefly outline the stages of SIT. For a 10- or 12-mark question (5 or 6 AO1 marks), you would need to provide more detail of each stage.

Meichenbaum's stress inoculation therapy

Conceptualisation: the client is encouraged by the therapist to identify the main sources of stress in their lives. This involves thinking back to stressful situations and how they turned out.

Skills training and rehearsal: the therapist helps the person to acquire skills that help them to cope with stressful situations. For instance, social anxiety (fear of social groups) is surprisingly common and very stressful. Sufferers may be poor at interacting with others, and this can be improved by helping them appear more approachable by social skills training. If exams are a key source of stress, training can be given in good study and revision habits. Relaxation training is always used in this stage, as the ability to calm down helps in all stressful situations.

Application in the real world: the skills and relaxation training are transferred to the real world. However, the client and therapist continue to monitor the success or failure of the training, and further training can be given if necessary.

SIT evaluation

- SIT begins by identifying the sources and causes of stress and then developing skills to help cope with them. So, if the therapy is successful, it provides a long-term solution to stress management.

- It takes time, motivation, commitment and money. Therefore, it is not suitable for or available to everyone.

- It has been shown to be effective in managing examination stress and other life stresses (Berger, 2000; Meichenbaum, 1985).

AQA Examiner's tip

Look up research evidence for SIT and identify its strengths and limitations. You might be required to evaluate SIT as a method of stress management.

Drugs: a physiological method of stress management

Symptoms of stress include high levels of anxiety and physiological arousal. Drugs have been developed to target these symptoms, and they have become some of the most prescribed drugs in the world.

Benzodiazepines

Benzodiazepines (BZs) are a class of anti-anxiety drugs used in the management of stress. Examples include Librium and Valium. BZs act in the brain on pathways using the neurotransmitter serotonin, and reduce feelings of anxiety and stress (Guidotti *et al.*, 1990).

- They do not work for everyone. Up to 40 per cent of people do not respond to BZ therapy.
- They need to be taken over weeks. They have a range of side effects, including memory problems, tiredness and loss of coordination (Stevens and Pollack, 2005).
- They can lead to physical dependence, meaning that when someone tries to come off BZs, they may suffer withdrawal symptoms.
- They do not target the causes of stress. At best they are a method of managing the symptoms of short-term stress, such as bereavement or divorce.

Beta-blockers

These drugs, such as propranolol, do not easily penetrate the brain, but they have a direct action on the heart and circulatory system of the body.

- They reduce heart rate and blood pressure and are very valuable treatments for the raised blood pressure (hypertension) associated with stress.
- Because they can act quickly they are the treatment of choice for life-threatening hypertension (Wilhelmsen *et al.*, 1987).
- Beta-blockers do not have major side effects as they do not enter the brain. They reduce stress-related arousal, but they do *not* target the causes of stress. Drugs are not a long-term solution to managing stress. Psychological methods should be used to provide long-term stress management, but they may be combined with drug therapy to control the symptoms of stress, especially in the early stages.

Think about it

Students often think that evaluation always means criticisms and limitations. In fact *positive* evaluation is almost always possible. Do not forget that all methods of stress management have problems, but they have been introduced because they can be effective.

AQA Examiner's tip

If you panic and forget the names of drugs used in stress management, do not worry. Examiners are more interested in your understanding in how they are used in stress management, and their strengths and limitations.

Quick test questions

1 Which three of the following are part of the pituitary-adrenal axis?

- [ ] Adrenocorticotrophic hormone
- [ ] Adrenal medulla
- [ ] Adrenaline
- [ ] Adrenal cortex
- [ ] Corticosteroids

2 In Kiecolt-Glaser *et al.*'s (1984) study of immune function in students taking exams, immune function was most reduced in students who also reported:

- [ ] High levels of depression
- [ ] High levels of anxiety
- [ ] High levels of Type A behaviour
- [ ] High levels of social isolation
- [ ] High levels of hostility

3 Chronic (long-term) stress weakens the whole immune system. This is called:

- [ ] Natural immunity
- [ ] Specific immunity
- [ ] Global immunosuppression
- [ ] Immunodeficiency
- [ ] Immune reactivity

4 Rahe *et al.* (1970) found a correlation of +0.118 between life event stress and illness outcomes. This is a:

- [ ] High negative correlation
- [ ] Low negative correlation
- [ ] Low positive correlation
- [ ] High positive correlation
- [ ] Moderate negative correlation

5 In Marmot *et al.*'s (1997) study on workplace stress, the most significant factor correlated with heart disease was:

- [ ] High workload
- [ ] High control over workload
- [ ] Obesity
- [ ] Low control over workload
- [ ] Smoking

6 Which three of the following are characteristics of Type A behaviour?

- [ ] Time pressure
- [ ] High levels of control
- [ ] Competitiveness
- [ ] High levels of commitment
- [ ] Hostility

7 Which three of the following are characteristics of hardiness?

- [ ] Control
- [ ] Competitiveness
- [ ] Challenge
- [ ] Hostility
- [ ] Commitment

8 Which three of the following can be applied to stress inoculation therapy?

- [ ] It targets the source of stress.
- [ ] It is quick and cheap.
- [ ] It involves acquiring new skills.
- [ ] It is suitable for everyone.
- [ ] It can provide long-term strategies for stress management.

Exam-style questions

As mentioned in the introduction, there are a variety of question styles, which require you to use material differently. Marks available can range from 1 to 12. You must read each question carefully, follow the requirements, and write enough to access the marks available.

Knowledge questions

1   Here are some important terms from the stress topic. What is meant by each of these?

Pituitary-adrenal system; Life changes; Daily hassles; Workplace stress; Type A behaviour; Hardiness; Stress inoculation therapy

2   Outline characteristics of Type A behaviour. *(2 marks)*

3   Outline the main features of the sympathomedullary pathway. *(3 marks)*

4   Outline what is meant by emotion-focused coping. *(2 marks)*

5   Explain the difference between life changes and daily hassles. *(3 marks)*

Apply it

For each term write a definition worth 2 marks. This requires a simple definition plus some brief elaboration. Now develop this definition into one worth 3 marks. Note that for some terms, such as life changes and problem-focused coping, examples are an effective method of elaboration.

AQA Examiner's tip

When asked to explain a difference between two things, note that it is not enough to simply list characteristics of each. You must explain clearly the underlying differences, e.g. how life changes are less common, or how daily hassles seem more related to illness.

Application questions

1   Mr Harris is about to move his business into a brand new building. He is very keen to create a healthy working environment and reduce workplace stress. In this way, he hopes to improve productivity and reduce absenteeism.

What advice would you give Mr Harris? Use your knowledge of psychological research in this area. *(6 marks)*

January 2010

AQA Examiner's tip

Remember that each piece of advice you give Mr Harris needs to be supported by research evidence, e.g. Marmot *et al*'s (1997) study suggests that low levels of personal control and high workloads can be very stressful. Focus on factors where you can quote research, and make sure that you do provide advice for Mr Harris.

2   Mary and Sophia are friends. Mary has to help her parents care for her grandmother, who lives with them but has severe arthritis and stays in bed most of the time. Mary's parents both have evening jobs so Mary has to look after her grandmother every evening after school, and then do her homework after her parents return. Sophia is worried about Mary, as recently Mary has had a series of coughs and colds and cannot shake them off.

Using your knowledge of psychology, explain why Mary might be vulnerable to coughs and colds.   *(4 marks)*

AQA   **Examiner's tip**

Begin by explaining that vulnerability to coughs and colds indicates an impaired immune system. Then link information in the scenario to research evidence, e.g. Mary is now a long-term carer. Kiecolt-Glaser *et al.* (1984) have shown that the stress of long-term caring can reduce the effectiveness of the immune system, leaving people vulnerable to illness.

AQA   **Examiner's tip**

For application questions, look for clues in the scenario. It may help to underline these. For top marks you should also refer directly to the scenario, and not simply write a general answer.

3   Derek suffers from severe examination stress. He finds it hard to focus on his work and cannot concentrate on revision because he is so anxious. He is worried that his exam results will suffer if he cannot work more effectively.

Explain how stress inoculation therapy could be used to help Derek and reduce his examination stress.   *(6 marks)*

AQA   **Examiner's tip**

Recall the three stages of stress inoculation therapy and apply them specifically to Derek's examination stress. Remember to provide enough detail to access all six marks, e.g. by naming and briefly elaborating on each of the stages.

Essay-style questions

1   Discuss research into stress-related illness and the immune system.
                                                        (12 marks)

2   Outline and evaluate the role of personality factors in responses to stress.   *(10 marks)*

3   Discuss two or more methods of stress management.   *(12 marks)*

Sample answers

Outline and evaluate one or more biological method of stress management.

(12 marks)

Drugs are a biological method of stress management. The most common drugs are benzodiazepines (BZs) and beta-blockers. BZs act in the brain on the neurotransmitter serotonin and help reduce the stress response. Beta-blockers do not enter the brain. They act on the body and control arousal by directly reducing heart rate and blood pressure. Drugs always have side effects. For instance BZs can affect memory and cause sleepiness, while beta-blockers can make respiratory problems like asthma worse. Drugs can also have problems of dependence and addiction. This has been a serious problem with BZs as they act in the brain. They should only be prescribed for a few weeks at a time.

However, drugs can be very effective at reducing responses to stress, and BZs have been the most prescribed drugs over the last 40 years. Beta-blockers can rapidly reduce high blood pressure which can be life-threatening. However, drugs only treat the symptoms of stress without changing the conditions that might be causing it, such as workplace stressors or life events. So they are best used in the short term. It is also recommended that they should be used together with psychological methods, such as stress inoculation therapy, which target the causes of stress.

Drugs are very convenient, quite cheap and can act quickly and are the most common form of stress management. However, they are not a cure as they only tackle symptoms. Psychological methods should be used to provide a long-term solution.

Reasonable detail on how drugs work, and good awareness of two classes of drugs

Concise evaluation of drug treatment. Each point has some elaboration and examples that demonstrate sound understanding.

Good point, but not entirely clear. Should mention that CBT takes a long time but drugs can help in the short term.

Slightly repetitive closing paragraph

AQA — Examiner's comments

This is a good answer. The outline of drug therapy is reasonably detailed and evaluation is thorough. Limitations are covered particularly well, with most points given some brief elaboration to show genuine understanding, and there is also a sensible section on the positive aspects of drug therapy. The answer becomes slightly repetitive at the end, but overall it is well organised and reasonably balanced, demonstrating good understanding. It would receive a mark towards the top band.

Outline research into workplace stress. (*6 marks*)

Research has identified many sources of workplace stress, including workload, control, and having to balance home and work. Karasek's model says that most stress is found when there is high workload but low control over the work. Marmot studied civil servants over eight years. He looked at lifestyle factors and sources of stress in the workplace. He found that the workers in the lowest grades had more chance of having heart attacks, and the most important factor was level of personal control over workload. This is supported by Johansson's study of the Swedish sawmill, where workers with high levels of responsibility but low control were most stressed. This research suggests that giving workers more control over their workloads can reduce levels of stress even when workloads are high.

Karasek's model is the product of research and is therefore acceptable.

Excellent brief summary of Marmot *et al.*'s study. Procedural detail helps understanding of findings

AQA Examiner's comments

This answer is focused and reasonably detailed for a 6-mark question. The term 'research' includes theory and studies, so Karasek's model is directly relevant. One study is then outlined in reasonable and accurate detail, and the findings supported by reference to other studies. Implications of the research at the end are a direct outcome of the studies quoted and would receive credit. This is an impressive answer and would receive marks in the top band.

AQA Examiner's tip

Where possible, refer to research studies in your answers to demonstrate your psychological knowledge and to support your statements. However, unless asked specifically about how the research was done, focus on findings and implications of findings. This demonstrates your understanding of psychological research.

5 Social psychology

Social influence

Types of conformity

> **You need to know how to**
>
> ✔ describe types of conformity, including compliance and internalisation
>
> ✔ explain the difference between them and identify examples in scenario questions.

Conformity

Conformity involves changing behaviour or what we think or say, because of the influence of or pressure from other people. This pressure can be real or imagined.

Conformity often occurs when one person changes their behaviour to fit in with a larger group of people (this is called **majority influence**).

Examples of conformity include starting to listen to a particular type of music or starting to smoke because your friends do.

> **Apply it**
>
> Think of a new example for compliance and one for internalisation.

Different types of conformity

	Description	Example	Explanation
Compliance	Shallow conformity: person conforms out loud with the views or behaviour but secretly disagrees	Phil laughs at a joke that others are laughing at but privately does not find it funny.	People usually comply because they do not want to stand out and look different. They may also comply to gain group acceptance.
Internalisation	Deep conformity: person is persuaded by the arguments and takes them on board both publicly and privately	Jane becomes a vegetarian at university when sharing a flat with other vegetarians. She is persuaded that eating meat is cruel and she keeps these views.	People internalise the views of others when they are convinced the arguments make sense or are 'right'.

Explanations of why people conform

> **You need to know how to**
>
> ✔ explain the main reasons why people conform, including normative social influence and informational social influence
>
> ✔ describe and evaluate research studies on conformity.

The dual-process model

The dual-process model gives **two reasons** why people conform.

Normative social influence

Conformity is based on the need to be accepted.

People conform because they want to be accepted and liked by a group of people who could make life difficult for them. This is shown in Asch's line experiment.

Informational social influence

Conformity is based on the need to be right.

People conform because they are unsure how to behave in a situation, or unsure what they think about an issue. This is shown in Sherif's light experiment.

AQA Examiner's tip

You need to know these key terms and you should be able to give your own examples of each. You can use the experiments by Asch and Sherif to show your understanding of normative and informational social influence.

Asch's experiments

Students were placed in groups and asked to match two sets of lines on cards. The other members of the group were confederates (in on the experiment) who all gave the same, wrong answer on some trials (called critical trials). On 37% of the critical trials those tested conformed with the wrong answers; 5% of the participants conformed in every critical trial; 25% refused to conform.

People conformed even when they knew the answer given by others was wrong.

In later versions of the experiment, Asch manipulated the size of the group of confederates. He found that conformity increased rapidly up to three confederates and did not increase much after that.

Sherif's experiment

Participants were asked to estimate how far a stationary spot of light moved in a dark room (an optical illusion). They were then placed in groups of three and repeated the task. Participants changed their original answers when they were in the group task to fit in with other people in their group.

People conformed because they were unsure, so they looked to others for the correct answer.

In studies based on Sherif's method, Rohrer found that, when re-tested one year later, people continued to conform to the norm of the group that they were in originally.

AQA Examiner's tip

You should be able to evaluate the dual-process model of conformity, for example by reference to relevant studies.

The dual-process model suggests that people conform because they depend on the group. However, this does not explain why people might continue to conform when other group members are no longer present. In Sherif's experiment, people still conformed to group estimates one year later when no other group members were present.

Referent social influence (social identity theory)

A further explanation of conformity is referent social influence. This explanation is based on an important theory in social psychology called social identity theory (SIT).

Social identity theory

An important part of a person's identity is their membership of different social groups (such as student, female, Londoner, etc.).

We see ourselves as similar to others in our group and different to people from different groups. This can lead us to be prejudiced towards other people.

The group provides us with rules and norms about how to behave. These rules are internalised and we use them to regulate our behaviour.

Hogg and Turner's (1987) experiments

Hogg and Turner carried out a series of experiments using a conformity task similar to Asch's 'line' experiment. Participants heard the responses of others, but gave their responses privately in a booth so others could not see or hear them. This meant that they did not need to worry about gaining group approval or feeling silly by disagreeing with other people.

- In one condition, the participant was with a group of confederates who were friends.
- In the second condition, they were placed with confederates who were strangers.

Hogg and Turner found that participants only conformed to false beliefs in the condition where they heard the views of their friends. This suggests that friends served as a reference group even though no one could see the answers the participant gave.

Asch, Sherif and Hogg and Turner all chose to use laboratory experiments to study conformity. However, in Sherif's experiment, there was no correct answer to the question as the light did not really move! This made it difficult to know whether participants were really conforming to group estimates or if the answers they gave were their own views.

Asch used a simple, unambiguous task – matching line lengths – so it would be obvious when participants were conforming. Asch used confederates to give the same, wrong answer and kept other variables constant. This allowed Asch to measure conformity (the dependent variable) easily, by noting whether the real participant gave the same wrong answer as the confederates. The method was adapted by Hogg and Turner to investigate the importance of group membership in conformity.

Advantages and disadvantages of the laboratory setting in studying conformity

Advantages	Disadvantages
Establishing cause and effect In each of these studies, the researchers manipulated an independent variable to assess its effect on a dependent variable.	**Lack of ecological validity** Asch's line task was unlike a real conformity situation in several ways. The correct answer was obvious, but in real-life conformity situations there is often no right answer. The line task was not important to the participants to get right, and people may be less likely to conform when something matters to them. Participants were among strangers and much real-life conformity takes place with friends or family.
High levels of control For example, Asch was able to control the task and the responses of the confederates. This made it easy to see when people conformed and to measure how many people conformed.	
Easy replication Rohrer replicated Sherif's experiment years later.	**Demand characteristics** In lab experiments, participants know they are being investigated and may become suspicious of the set-up.

Think about it

You can use this explanation of conformity to criticise the dual-process model. Referent social influence can explain why people continue to conform even when group members are not present. Normative social influence assumes that we conform to be accepted, but only when group members are present and can see.

Apply it

Work out the independent and dependent variables in the conformity experiments.

Think about it

Not everyone conformed in Asch's experiment. Twenty-five per cent of people kept their own viewpoint and remained independent. This shows that individual differences are important in understanding conformity.

Asch's experiment was carried out in the US in the 1950s, a time known as the 'McCarthy era', when conformity was much more common than today. Later studies (Perrin and Spencer, 1981) have shown much lower rates of conformity.

Ethical issues

Almost all conformity studies involve deception: if people knew conformity was being studied, they would be unlikely to conform. Asch's study shows a lack of informed consent. Participants were deceived and were subjected to mild levels of stress and embarrassment. This is unlikely to have caused lasting damage.

Obedience

> ### You need to know how to
> ✔ explain what is meant by obedience
> ✔ describe and evaluate Milgram's original research into obedience and the variations on his original study.

Obedience is doing what you are told. It involves complying with an order to do something, usually given by someone with power (e.g. boss, teacher).

Key study

The work of Milgram: original study (1963)

Sample: Milgram used an advert in a local paper to recruit 40 male volunteers. Each was paid $4.50 to take part in a study of 'punishment and learning'.

Method: Participants arrived separately at Yale University and were introduced to a confederate of Milgram. They believed that this person was another participant. Lots were drawn. The real participant was given the role of teacher, and the confederate had the role of learner. The 'teacher' was told to give an electric shock to the learner in the next room every time he got a question wrong in a memory test. The shocks started at 15 volts and increased in 15 V steps to a maximum of 450 V.

Controls: The learner's screams and shouts were pre-recorded. At 180 V, the learner complained of a weak heart and at 300 V he demanded to leave. The experimenter used a set of standard prompts ('You must continue' and 'The experiment requires you to continue') to put pressure on the participants to continue.

Findings: Despite showing signs of stress, protesting verbally and arguing, all 40 participants went up to 300 V. Sixty-five per cent went to the full 450 V.

Conclusion: Milgram concluded from his study that ordinary people can do extraordinary things when put under pressure in situations like his experiment.

> **AQA** Examiner's tip
>
> You may be asked directly about Milgram's studies in the exam as they are mentioned in the Specification.

> **Think about it**
>
> Milgram's variations tell us a lot about why people choose to obey or disobey orders.

Variations on Milgram's basic study

Milgram carried out 18 further experiments, using the same basic method, to investigate factors that influence obedience. These variations tell us about why people may choose to obey or disobey an order in different situations.

Variations on Milgram's basic study (percentage going to 450 V)

- Moving the experiment from Yale University to a downtown office (48 per cent)
- Making the teacher give the orders over the phone (20 per cent)
- Providing a confederate who disobeyed the orders (10 per cent)

These factors **reduced the authority** of the person giving the order.

- Bringing the learner into the same room as the teacher (30 per cent)
- Forcing the learner's hand onto the shock plate (30 per cent)

These factors brought the teacher into **closer contact** with the learner so they could see his pain.

Criticisms of Milgram's research

Milgram's research into obedience generated considerable discussion at the time and continues to do so nearly 50 years after his experiments were carried out. Some of the most important criticisms of Milgram's work are covered here.

Examiner's tip

You do not need to recall the exact percentages of obedience in these variations.

Baumrind (1964) made the following ethical criticisms of Milgram's research

Baumrind's criticisms	Milgram's responses
Milgram deceived his participants and did not inform them of the nature of the research.	Milgram argued that he gained presumptive consent by asking psychologists and psychiatrists before the study what would happen.
Participants were prevented from withdrawing from the experiment.	Milgram argued that people *could* withdraw even though it was difficult – and 35 per cent did by refusing to give the full shocks.
Participants were put in a stressful situation, which could have harmed them emotionally.	Milgram argued that he debriefed his participants, immediately afterwards, and followed up 1,000 with a questionnaire. He also employed an independent psychiatrist to check them for harm one year later.

Orne and Holland (1968) criticised Milgram's experiments for a lack of validity

Orne and Holland's criticisms	Milgram's response
Orne and Holland claimed that Milgram's participants did not believe that the shocks were real. Participants would have worked out that there was no need for a 'teacher'. Milgram could have simply given the shocks himself to punish the learner if the experiment was about punishment.	Milgram argued that his participants were fooled by the procedure and believed the shocks were real.
Orne and Holland argued that participants realised that the experiment was a set-up and gave the shocks knowing they would not hurt anyone.	He drew attention to the film footage of the experiment, which showed the extreme stress experienced by many of his participants who sweated, stuttered and burst into nervous laughter.
If this criticism was true, it would seriously undermine Milgram's research as it would be a meaningless test of obedience.	

David Mandel (1998) has argued that Milgram's experiments have provided an 'obedience alibi' for people accused of war crimes. The findings of his experiment suggest that ordinary people can do extraordinary – and potentially evil – things when put under pressure by authority figures. Historical figures such as Adolf Eichmann and William Calley have argued that they should not be held responsible for acts as they were simply obeying orders.

Why do people obey?

You need to know how to

✔ explain the main situational factors that lead to obedience.

Milgram's experiment showed a high level of obedience – all 40 participants went to 300V and 65 per cent went to 450V. Milgram identified *situational* factors as the main reason why ordinary people obeyed.

Factors influencing obedience

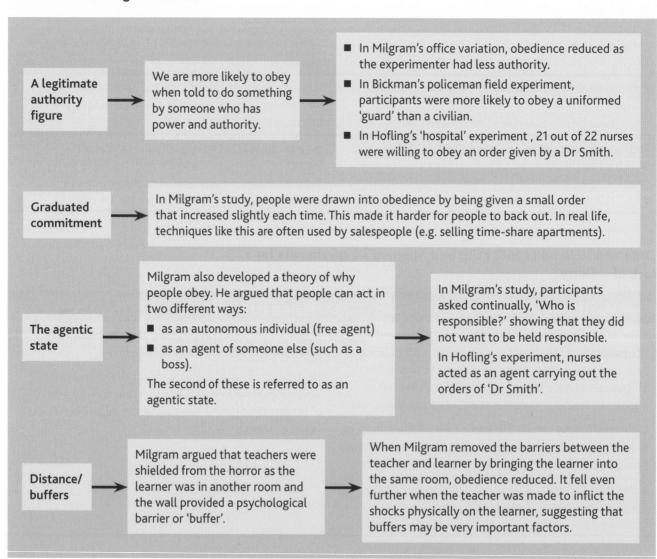

A legitimate authority figure → We are more likely to obey when told to do something by someone who has power and authority. →
- In Milgram's office variation, obedience reduced as the experimenter had less authority.
- In Bickman's policeman field experiment, participants were more likely to obey a uniformed 'guard' than a civilian.
- In Hofling's 'hospital' experiment , 21 out of 22 nurses were willing to obey an order given by a Dr Smith.

Graduated commitment → In Milgram's study, people were drawn into obedience by being given a small order that increased slightly each time. This made it harder for people to back out. In real life, techniques like this are often used by salespeople (e.g. selling time-share apartments).

The agentic state → Milgram also developed a theory of why people obey. He argued that people can act in two different ways:
- as an autonomous individual (free agent)
- as an agent of someone else (such as a boss).

The second of these is referred to as an agentic state. → In Milgram's study, participants asked continually, 'Who is responsible?' showing that they did not want to be held responsible.
In Hofling's experiment, nurses acted as an agent carrying out the orders of 'Dr Smith'.

Distance/ buffers → Milgram argued that teachers were shielded from the horror as the learner was in another room and the wall provided a psychological barrier or 'buffer'. → When Milgram removed the barriers between the teacher and learner by bringing the learner into the same room, obedience reduced. It fell even further when the teacher was made to inflict the shocks physically on the learner, suggesting that buffers may be very important factors.

Social influence in everyday life

Explanations of independent behaviour

> **You need to know how to**
>
> explain what is meant by independent behaviour
>
> explain the situational factors that influence whether or not people are able to resist pressures to conform or obey.

Independent behaviour occurs when someone resists the pressure to conform or refuses to obey an order.

What proportion of people, according to the studies, show independent behaviour?

- In Asch's study of conformity, 25 per cent of participants remained independent and did not conform.
- In Milgram's original study of obedience, 35 per cent resisted the order to give 450V shocks.
- In Hofling's study of nurses, 1 out of 22 disobeyed the instruction to give a drug to a patient.

Milgram's studies have shown the powerful role of situational forces in obedience. They also highlight the kinds of factors that make people more likely to *challenge authority* and behave independently.

> **Apply it**
>
> Think about real-life situations that resemble Milgram's variations – e.g. when someone is given an order by a boss at work.
>
> The last variations is fairly unlikely to happen to most people in real-life situations, except perhaps those in the armed forces.

Milgram study: variations and effect on obedience

Variation (% going to 450V)	Why it lead to more disobedience
Run-down office condition (48 per cent)	The person giving the orders had less authority and social power. People with less power are less likely to punish us.
Teacher gives orders over the phone (20 per cent)	It is easier to disobey orders when the person who gave them is not there, perhaps because we cannot see their disapproval or hope they might not find out.
Confederate who disobeys teacher's orders (10 per cent)	It is easier to disobey someone when other people have done this as we can conform with their behaviour.
Learner in same room as teacher (30 per cent)	It is harder to do something unpleasant face to face, when we can see our behaviour producing unpleasant consequences for someone. For example, many people can write unpleasant comments about someone online that they would not say to the person's face.
Teacher made to force learner's hand onto shock plate (30 per cent)	It is very difficult for most people to physically inflict pain on other people.

Individual differences in independent behaviour and locus of control

You need to know how to

✔ explain how people vary in their tendency to conform, obey or remain independent

✔ explain how locus of control influences conformity and independent behaviour.

Milgram's studies have shown how, in some situations, people are more likely to resist obeying orders. However, people as individuals also differ in how generally obedient or conformist they are. Some of this is related to upbringing. Adorno suggested that childhood experiences are crucial in creating obedient people. One of Milgram's disobedient participants was Gretchen Brandt, a survivor of the Nazi death camps. An important personality factor in independent behaviour is locus of control.

Locus of control (LC)

LC is measured using a multi-item questionnaire that produces a score indicating an internal or external locus of control.

People with an **internal locus of control** believe strongly that they are in control of their own lives and they can alter what happens.

People with an **external locus of control** believe strongly that most things are outside their control. Control of their lives may be with their parents, the government, fate or the stars.

Think about it

Where might a person's locus of control come from? How could it relate to childhood experiences and upbringing?

Findings about independent and obedient people

Obedient people	Independent people
Some studies have suggested that more obedient people have an external locus of control (ELC).	Less obedient/more independent people have an internal locus of control (ILC).
Avtgis (1998) found that people with an ELC were more easily persuaded and more likely to conform.	Oliner and Oliner (1988) interviewed 406 Germans who had sheltered Jews from the Nazis. They scored more highly on social responsibility and had an ILC.
However, Williams and Warchal (1981) found that conformers were less assertive but did not score differently to non-conformers on an LC test.	Elms and Milgram (1974) found that disobedient participants in Milgram's original experiment had higher scores on social responsibility and ILC.

Social change

> **You need to know how to**
>
> ✓ explain what is meant by social change and give real examples of social change
>
> ✓ explain how social influence research can help to explain social change
>
> ✓ explain how minority influence can bring about social change.

Social change refers to changes in attitudes, behaviours or laws that take place on a large scale and effect society.

Groups of people can encourage others to change their behaviour to fit in or conform. Single individuals or small groups can also persuade the majority to accept their views (minority influence). This is important in social change.

Some examples of social change

- The suffragette movement in the UK campaigned and won women the right to vote in the 1920s.
- The civil rights movement in the US brought about equal rights for black Americans in the 1960s.
- Gay rights group Stonewall achieved the legalisation of homosexual relationships between men and the right to civil partnerships.

How social change happens

- Social change occurs through *minority influence*. Moscovici (1969) carried out a laboratory experiment with two conditions. In the first, a minority group of two people inconsistently called a set of blue slides 'green'. This had little effect on the majority who continued to call them blue. However, in the second condition, the minority group called *all* of the slides green and around 10 per cent of the majority group changed to adopt this view. This shows the importance of presenting a consistent argument such as that used by the suffragettes to gain the vote for women.
- Clark's (1998/99) mock jury study of the film *12 Angry Men* showed how people begin to change their minds when they can see others adopting the minority viewpoint or defecting. This is sometimes called the *snowball effect*. The snowball effect occurred during the civil rights movement as people moved towards the view that black people should be given the right to vote.
- Most social change comes about through *social action*. Rosa Parks' defiant action of sitting in the 'whites only' area of a bus in the USA sparked a series of riots and protests. However, minority groups can also use *social creativity* (e.g. the 'Black is beautiful' campaign), where groups redefine themselves more positively.

Apply it

Research some examples of social action taken by key activists such as Emmeline Pankhurst, Emily Davidson, Nelson Mandela and Rosa Parks. What changes were achieved and what strategies were used to change public opinion?

AQA Examiner's tip

Remember that acting independently is the first step in social change. You can use your knowledge of social influence and independent behaviour to help explain social change.

AQA Examiner's tip

Make sure that you can explain examples of social change by referring to research studies such as that of Moscovici (1969).

Quick test questions

1 Choose one of the following to complete the statement:

Normative social influence involves conforming because

- ☐ the person giving the order has authority/power
- ☐ we do not know how to behave so we copy other people
- ☐ we want to fit in and be liked by the group
- ☐ we will be punished if we do not conform
- ☐ we like the people we are conforming with

2 Which two of the following are not explanations of conformity?

- ☐ Agentic state
- ☐ Informational social influence
- ☐ Authoritarian personality
- ☐ Referent social influence
- ☐ Normative social influence

3 Which of the following statements are untrue of Milgram's research into obedience?

- ☐ The experiment took place at Yale University.
- ☐ The shock generator ran from 15V to 600V.
- ☐ Participants were prompted to continue.
- ☐ Milgram carried out a replication of his study in a downtown office.
- ☐ Half of the participants went to 450V.

4 Which of the following factors led to high levels of obedience in Milgram's experiment?

- ☐ Participants could not see the pain of the learner due to 'buffers'.
- ☐ The orders came from a legitimate authority figure.
- ☐ The orders were given by a man wearing a guard's uniform.
- ☐ The participants were threatened with violence.
- ☐ The shocks started at a low level and went up slowly in stages.

5 Which of the following ethical criticisms have been made of Milgram's research into obedience? (Tick several)

- ☐ Milgram deceived his participants.
- ☐ Milgram did not debrief his participants.
- ☐ Milgram put his participants under emotional stress.
- ☐ Milgram did not get informed consent.
- ☐ Milgram did not follow up his participants to check for harm.

6 Which of the following are explanations why some people are less obedient/more independent than others?

- ☐ Less obedient people have an internal locus of control.
- ☐ Less obedient people have an external locus of control.
- ☐ Less obedient people have an authoritarian personality.
- ☐ Less obedient people have a strong sense of social responsibility.
- ☐ Less obedient people were not punished enough when they were children.

7 An 'agentic state' occurs when:

- ☐ the psychologist carries out studies in disguise
- ☐ people obey because they do not see themselves as responsible for their actions
- ☐ people become stressed and frightened by taking part in research
- ☐ people obey because they are afraid of consequences
- ☐ people are paid to carry out orders

8 Which two processes are important in social change?

- ☐ The snowball effect
- ☐ Social influence
- ☐ Minority influence
- ☐ The dual-process model
- ☐ Social identity theory

Exam-style questions

There are different kinds of exam questions, which require you to use material differently. Marks available can range from 1 to 12. You must read each question carefully, follow the requirements and write enough to access the marks available.

Knowledge questions

1   Here are some important terms from the social influence topic. Explain what is meant by each of these:

Conformity; Compliance; Internalisation; Normative social influence; Informational social influence; Obedience; Independent behaviour; Social change; Locus of control

2   Explain the difference between compliance and internalisation.
                                                    (*3 marks*)

3   Explain the difference between normative social influence and informational social influence.   (*3 marks*)

4   Outline two explanations of obedience.   (*2 marks + 2 marks*)

5   Outline two explanations of conformity.   (*2 marks + 2 marks*)

Application questions

1   Sam has just started a new job in a shop. She notices that the rest of her new workmates are late leaving the staff room at the end of breaks and regularly stretch their break time from 10 to 15 minutes. Sam does not think this is a good idea but goes along with her new colleagues. Explain Sam's behaviour in terms of compliance.
                                                    (*2 marks*)

2   Peter is driving home late at night when a man steps into the road and signals for him to stop. Peter carries on driving but a short while later is asked to stop by a policeman who uses the same gestures. Peter immediately stops the car and gets out. Using your knowledge of the psychology of obedience, explain why Peter stops when asked by the policeman but not when asked by the first man.   (*3 marks*)

3   For many years, smoking in public places such as trains, pubs and restaurants was quite acceptable. People could smoke wherever they wanted and non-smokers had to put up with smoky atmospheres. However, in 2007, the government finally introduced a law banning smoking in public places, and those who smoke are limited to where they can smoke. Using your knowledge of the psychology of social change, explain how this social change has occurred.   (*4 marks*)

June 2010

Apply it

Remember to look at the number of marks allocated to decide how much depth and detail you need in your answer. Try writing 2-mark definitions for each of these terms in the first question. Then try to develop your answers into 3-mark definitions.

AQA **Examiner's tip**

For application questions, remember to look for the clues in the scenario. It may help to underline these.

Methodological questions

1   (a) How have social psychologists investigated conformity?

(4 marks)

(b) Explain **one** methodological criticism of the method outlined in (a). *(2 marks)*

2   (a) How have psychologists investigated obedience? *(4 marks)*

(b) Explain **one** methodological criticism of the method outlined in (a). *(2 marks)*

3   (a) Milgram's work can be criticised for being unethical. Describe **one** way in which his work is unethical. *(2 marks)*

(b) Apart from ethical issues, give **one** strength and one limitation of Milgram's methodology. *(2 marks + 2 marks)*

> **AQA Examiner's tip**
>
> In 'How' questions, remember to state the method and to bring out aspects such as the IV and DV if it is an experiment.

Essay-style questions

1   Outline and evaluate explanations of obedience. *(12 marks)*

2   Outline and evaluate explanations of conformity. *(10 marks)*

3   Outline and evaluate criticisms of Milgram's research into obedience. *(10 marks)*

Sample answers

When a policeman is wearing a uniform and directing traffic, you are very likely to obey him. However, if you meet the same policeman but he is dressed in civilian clothes, you are less likely to obey him. Using your knowledge of obedience, explain why you are less likely to obey the plain-clothes policeman. *(4 marks)*

When a policeman wears a uniform, it provides a clear social symbol of his legitimate authority and social power. This means that he is likely to be obeyed as he has the power to punish people who disobey. However, in plain clothes, a policeman appears to have no more authority than an ordinary person, so he is less likely to be obeyed. This was shown in Bickman's study of obedience when people were much more obedient to the uniformed guard than the civilian.

The candidate has started well by referring to the scenario at the start of their answer.

A clear statement of why a uniform leads to obedience

Good linkage back to the scenario with reference to a research study to back up the point

AQA Examiner's comments

This answer engages well with the scenario, continually referring back to it.

There is reference to a piece of relevant research (Bickman) and to clear and accurate psychological knowledge of legitimate authority.

This answer would receive a mark in the top band.

Outline and evaluate reasons why people obey. *(12 marks)*

There are many different reasons why people might obey an order given. One of the most important is who gives the order/instruction. When an order is given by a legitimate authority figure people are far more likely to obey without question: this may be because they trust the authority figure OR because they may be punished for disobeying. This was shown in Milgram's classic obedience experiments. 65 per cent of people obeyed the order to administer a potentially fatal 450V shock when the experiment was carried out at Yale University. When it was moved to a downtown office obedience fell to 48 per cent as there was less trust in the source of authority. In Hofling's field study of nurses, 21/22 were willing to obey the unknown Doctor Smith. In everyday life, the amount of authority is very important in terms of obedience: people such as doctors and police hold lots of authority as shown in Bickman's study.

Another important reason why people obeyed in Milgram's experiment was the gradual nature of the task. Here, the shocks started at a low rate (15V) and went up in small steps to 450V. It is likely that more people would have refused if the shocks had started at a high level. However, it became difficult to back out having started by obeying and this may be why so many people continued. This may be important in real-life situations where demands start small but escalate – such as when people are blackmailed.

A final reason why people obey could be that they are obedient people. In Milgram's experiment the most obedient were those who had an authoritarian personality. Adorno suggests that a harsh upbringing where children are smacked makes them resent their parents but be obedient to other people. This is all very well but lots of people who are brought up this way go the other way and become disobedient and challenge authority. So this explanation is not as good as the others.

Start by naming the explanation – a legitimate authority figure giving the order. Keep description short and snappy. Two or three sentences will do the trick.

A good block of effective research evidence here. Note that there is not that much descriptive detail of the studies.

Apply the explanation to real-life situations/ examples

Second explanation – again short description

This comment is a weaker one than earlier situations/ examples application.

This last section is less appropriate. There are a couple of misunderstandings of Adorno's explanation of obedience.

AQA — Examiner's comments

This answer would achieve marks in the lower part of the top band.

The description of why people obey is less detailed but generally accurate. It demonstrates relevant knowledge and understanding.

For the evaluation of the reasons why people obey, the AO2 credit has been gained for citing evidence to support the reasons for obedience. There is some limited attempt to judge the reasons, but this could have been developed by considering the quality of the evidence (reliability, validity) and the material is not always used effectively.

6 Individual differences – psychopathology (abnormality)

Defining and explaining abnormality

Definitions of abnormality

> **You need to know how to**
>
> ✔ describe definitions of abnormality: deviation from social norms, failure to function adequately and deviation from ideal mental health
>
> ✔ explain the limitations of these definitions.

AQA Examiner's tip

Demonstrate your understanding of definitions of abnormality by using examples. Adjust the level of detail in your answer to the number of marks available. If you are asked to apply a definition to a scenario, make sure you do not talk just in general terms but apply your knowledge to the specific example in the scenario.

The terms 'psychopathology' or 'abnormality' refer to psychological disorders such as schizophrenia, depression and phobias. A major aim of psychology is to explain these disorders so that effective therapies can be developed. However, before we can study specific disorders, psychologists need to define how abnormal behaviour differs from normal behaviour. Several definitions of abnormality have been proposed.

Deviation from social norms (DSN)

Every society has commonly accepted rules of behaviour, or social norms, such as queuing politely or not standing too close to people when talking. Deviation from these norms can then be seen as evidence of abnormality. An example would be the person with obsessive-compulsive disorder who washes their hands 50 times a day.
However, the definition has limitations:

Deviations from social norms may simply be **eccentricity**, such as avoiding stepping on the cracks in the pavement. They can also depend on the context. Someone dressed as a giant rabbit looks like they are deviating from social norms, until you see that they are part of a charity walk.

Social norms vary across cultures. This is referred to as cultural relativity. Strolling naked around Nottingham would be seen by us as abnormal, but wearing a three-piece suit in the Amazonian jungle would be seen as a deviation from the social norms of Amazonian Indians.

Social norms change over time. Homosexuality was included as a clinical psychiatric disorder up until the 1960s, but social attitudes have now changed. So deviation from social norms as a definition of abnormality is era-dependent.

Criminal activity is a deviation from social norms, but in most cases we assume the person has free will and is responsible for their actions. So they are not classified as abnormal or psychologically disordered.

Failure to function adequately (FFA)

People not able to attain their normal pattern of behaviour are said to be failing to function adequately. Examples might be the depressed person who cannot hold down a job and whose relationships break up because of their depressed mood, or the agoraphobic who is afraid to leave their house.

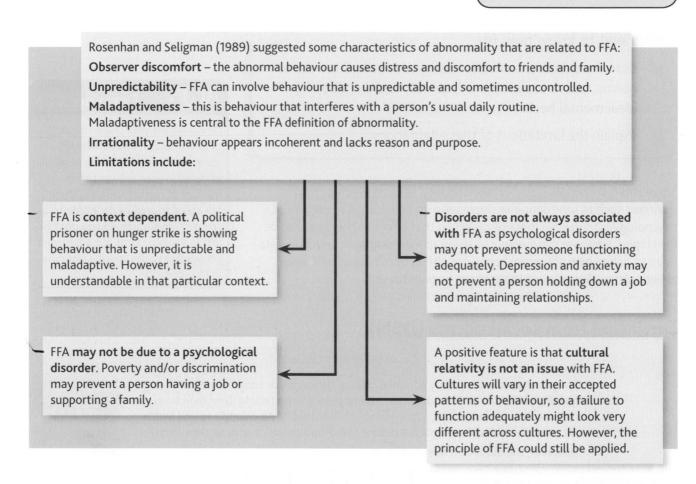

Rosenhan and Seligman (1989) suggested some characteristics of abnormality that are related to FFA:

Observer discomfort – the abnormal behaviour causes distress and discomfort to friends and family.

Unpredictability – FFA can involve behaviour that is unpredictable and sometimes uncontrolled.

Maladaptiveness – this is behaviour that interferes with a person's usual daily routine. Maladaptiveness is central to the FFA definition of abnormality.

Irrationality – behaviour appears incoherent and lacks reason and purpose.

Limitations include:

FFA is **context dependent**. A political prisoner on hunger strike is showing behaviour that is unpredictable and maladaptive. However, it is understandable in that particular context.

Disorders are not always associated with FFA as psychological disorders may not prevent someone functioning adequately. Depression and anxiety may not prevent a person holding down a job and maintaining relationships.

FFA **may not be due to a psychological disorder**. Poverty and/or discrimination may prevent a person having a job or supporting a family.

A positive feature is that **cultural relativity is not an issue** with FFA. Cultures will vary in their accepted patterns of behaviour, so a failure to function adequately might look very different across cultures. However, the principle of FFA could still be applied.

Deviation from ideal mental health (DIMH)

Introduced by Jahoda (1958), this is a different approach in that it tries to define what it is to be normal rather than abnormal. Then, abnormality becomes a failure to match these characteristics of normality. Features of ideal mental health include the following:

- A person should be in touch with their feelings.
- They should be resistant to stress.
- They should focus on the future and self-actualisation. Self-actualisation means that a person achieves their full potential in life.
- They should show empathy, that is understanding and sympathy towards others.

This is a very positive approach, emphasising that we should be striving for improvement. However, it is severely limited as an approach to abnormality.

- Cultural relativity is the main limitation. Jahoda's characteristics are very much based on Western individualistic values of personal growth and achievement, and would be hard to apply to collectivist cultures.

- DIMH represents deviation from an ideal state, and most of us would fail to match up to all of the characteristics. In that sense, most of us would be seen as abnormal. It is also unclear how far a person has to deviate before being defined as abnormal.

Diagnosis of specific psychological disorders uses detailed analysis of symptoms, along with a general assessment of the person's overall functioning. This assessment includes aspects of the deviation from social norms and failure to function adequately approaches to defining abnormality.

Explaining abnormality

> **You need to know how to**
>
> describe how the biological, psychodynamic, behavioural and cognitive approaches explain abnormality
>
> evaluate these approaches to psychopathology.

The biological approach to psychopathology

As its name implies, this approach focuses on the biology of the body, in particular the brain. It makes several assumptions.

AQA Examiner's tip

The Specification does not refer to specific disorders such as schizophrenia and depression. However, use of relevant examples is an excellent way to demonstrate your knowledge and understanding.

The biological approach to psychopathology

Assumptions

- All behaviour, normal and abnormal, is associated with changes in brain function.
- These changes may involve levels of brain neurotransmitters, or changes in brain structure.
- A significant genetic component is involved in most behaviours, including psychopathology. It is heavily on the nature side of the nature–nurture debate.

Examples of the biological approach

- Schizophrenia has been linked both to changes in brain structure and to increased levels of the neurotransmitter dopamine.
- Depression has been associated with low levels of the neurotransmitter serotonin.
- Twin and family studies indicate that there is a major genetic component in schizophrenia.

Evaluation of the biological approach

- The biological approach is supported by modern brain-scanning techniques. These have identified changes in neurotransmitters and brain structure in conditions such as schizophrenia and depression.
- Evidence shows that no disorder is 100 per cent caused by genetic factors. A popular model is diathesis-stress, where a genetic vulnerability (e.g. to schizophrenia) is triggered by environmental stress.
- Drugs targeting neurotransmitters can be very effective in treating conditions such as schizophrenia and depression.
- The approach is heavily reductionist. This means it assumes that explanations at the basic level of biology are all we need to explain psychopathology. It ignores higher-level factors such as social, environmental and cultural factors. Social factors such as poverty and social isolation, for instance, can be key factors in causing depression.

AQA Examiner's tip

A common mistake that students make is to refer to the biological approach as 'reductionist', without explaining what the term means and why it is relevant. To earn marks you must demonstrate your understanding of the terms you use, e.g. that the reductionist approach ignores psychological and cultural factors that may also cause psychological disorders.

The psychodynamic approach

This approach assumes that adult behaviour, normal and abnormal, reflects complex and dynamic interactions between conscious and unconscious processes from birth onwards. Freud's original theory has two key elements: a model of human personality, and a detailed stage theory of psychosexual development.

Apply it

As a revision exercise make a list of three key assumptions for each of the approaches to psychopathology listed in the specification. Make sure that the assumptions are related specifically to psychopathology (psychological disorders).

The **superego** is our conscience or sense of morality. It develops in the phallic stage of development through identification with our parents.

→ Superego dominance may lead to problems and guilt experiencing pleasure, and the development of adult anxiety and depression.

The **ego** represents our conscious self. It develops through early childhood and tries to balance the instinctual demands of the id for gratification and the moral rules provided by our superego. The ego operates on the **reality principle**.

→ If the ego fails to balance the competing demands of the id and superego, psychological disorders may result.

The **id**: this is a reservoir of unconscious and instinctive psychic energy, the libido. The id operates on the **pleasure principle** and constantly tries to gratify its instincts through sex and aggression.

→ Dominance of id impulses may lead to conduct disorders in children and aggressive disorders (e.g. psychopathy) in adults.

The psychodynamic structure of human personality
Stages of psychosexual development

At each stage the instinctual energy of the id looks for gratification in different bodily areas. If the child is over-gratified or deprived at any particular stage, fixation may result and lead to later psychological problems. Freud did not emphasise later stages of psychosexual development, such as latent and genital, as much as these early stages.

Stages of psychosexual development

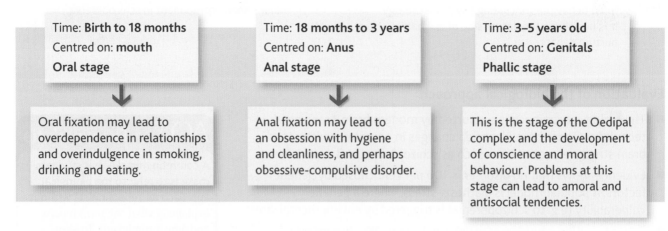

Time: **Birth to 18 months**
Centred on: **mouth**
Oral stage

↓

Oral fixation may lead to overdependence in relationships and overindulgence in smoking, drinking and eating.

Time: **18 months to 3 years**
Centred on: **Anus**
Anal stage

↓

Anal fixation may lead to an obsession with hygiene and cleanliness, and perhaps obsessive-compulsive disorder.

Time: **3–5 years old**
Centred on: **Genitals**
Phallic stage

↓

This is the stage of the Oedipal complex and the development of conscience and moral behaviour. Problems at this stage can lead to amoral and antisocial tendencies.

Defence mechanisms are used by the ego to protect itself against the anxiety caused by conflicts between the id and the superego, or by unresolved conflicts at psychosexual stages. **Repression** into the unconscious is the best known. The aim of psychoanalysis is to overcome these defence mechanisms.

Evaluation of Freud's psychodynamic theories

- Freud was the first to emphasise the importance of unconscious processes in child and adult behaviour. It is now accepted that repression of painful childhood experiences can lead to adult disorders such as depression and anxiety.
- Freud did not study children directly. He worked with adults with neurotic disorders and then associated their problems with their early experiences.
- Basic Freudian concepts such as id, ego and superego are impossible to test using conventional scientific methods. They may not be wrong, but they cannot be validated.
- Freud worked in Vienna (Austria) in the late 19th and early 20th centuries. His views therefore reflect this historical and cultural period, e.g. its emphasis on repressed sexuality. However, Freud has influenced every major psychodynamic approach since then and is one of the most influential psychologists of all time.

> **AQA Examiner's tip**
>
> When evaluating Freud's work, students have a habit of providing only limitations. Do not forget that he also introduced some of the most significant insights into the role of early experience and of the unconscious into psychology.

The behavioural approach

The behavioural approach assumes that all normal and abnormal behaviour is produced through learning and experience. It makes several assumptions based on different forms of learning.

The behavioural approach

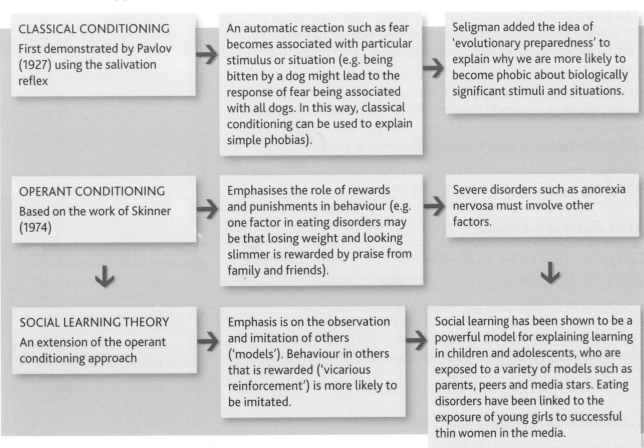

CLASSICAL CONDITIONING
First demonstrated by Pavlov (1927) using the salivation reflex

→ An automatic reaction such as fear becomes associated with particular stimulus or situation (e.g. being bitten by a dog might lead to the response of fear being associated with all dogs. In this way, classical conditioning can be used to explain simple phobias).

→ Seligman added the idea of 'evolutionary preparedness' to explain why we are more likely to become phobic about biologically significant stimuli and situations.

OPERANT CONDITIONING
Based on the work of Skinner (1974)

→ Emphasises the role of rewards and punishments in behaviour (e.g. one factor in eating disorders may be that losing weight and looking slimmer is rewarded by praise from family and friends).

→ Severe disorders such as anorexia nervosa must involve other factors.

SOCIAL LEARNING THEORY
An extension of the operant conditioning approach

→ Emphasis is on the observation and imitation of others ('models'). Behaviour in others that is rewarded ('vicarious reinforcement') is more likely to be imitated.

→ Social learning has been shown to be a powerful model for explaining learning in children and adolescents, who are exposed to a variety of models such as parents, peers and media stars. Eating disorders have been linked to the exposure of young girls to successful thin women in the media.

Evaluation of the behavioural approach

- The behavioural approach can provide convincing explanations of some disorders, such as the role of classical conditioning in phobias or of social learning in eating disorders. However, there is little evidence that disorders such as schizophrenia involve learning processes.

- Treatments based on the behavioural approach can be effective, especially for simple phobias. This provides some support for the model.

- The behavioural approach is reductionist in that it explains behaviour using simple learning principles. It ignores more complex influences such as cognitive and emotional factors in abnormal behaviour.

- The approach assumes that all behaviour is based on learning and experience. It has no role for genetic factors, and so is on the nurture side of the nature–nurture debate. There is clear evidence for an influence of genetic factors in some disorders.

The cognitive approach

The cognitive approach emphasises cognitive processes such as attention, perception and thoughts about the self and the world. Abnormal behaviour develops because of maladaptive and irrational cognitive processes.

- **Schemata** are organised ways of relating to ourselves and the world. For example, 'I am confident', 'I am good at relationships'.

- Unhappy experiences early in life may lead to the development of **negative schemata**: 'I am not loved', 'I will always be unsuccessful'.

- **Negative schemata** lead to **cognitive biases** in the way people see the world. In depression, for example, people interpret the world in a pessimistic way, ignoring positive events and so reinforcing their negative views.

Examples of **cognitive biases** include *minimising* the good things that happen, *maximising* the bad things that happen, and *all or nothing thinking*, in which life is black and white – you are a failure at everything, rather than, like most people, being good at some things and less good at others.

One of the most influential cognitive approaches is Beck's (1979) model of depression. This involves three negative schemata.

Beck's model of depression

Negative view of the self – 'I am a failure and do not deserve to be happy'

Negative view of the world – 'It is a hostile and unfriendly place'

Negative view of the future – 'There will always be problems, I will never be happy'

Evaluation of the cognitive approach

- There is research evidence for cognitive biases and maladaptive thinking in disorders such as depression and anxiety. For example, when asked to recall word lists, depressed participants recall more negative words than non-depressed participants (Burt *et al.*, 1995).

> ## Apply it
>
> The behavioural approach can seem quite complicated. There are no disorders listed in the specification, but a way to test your understanding is to apply the behavioural approach to disorders such as phobias. Use of such examples in the exam is also a highly effective demonstration of your knowledge and understanding.

> ## Apply it
>
> The cognitive approach can be hard to understand. Review the assumptions of the approach and make sure that you can demonstrate your understanding of these assumptions by referring to Beck's model.

- Treatments based on the cognitive approach (cognitive-behavioural therapy) can be very effective for disorders such as anxiety and depression. This gives some support to the approach.
- The cognitive approach ignores biological and genetic factors in psychopathology. But it is not reductionist as it takes a complex view of psychological disorders.

Treating abnormality

> **You need to know how to**
>
> ✔ describe and evaluate the use of biological therapies in treating abnormality
>
> ✔ describe and evaluate the use of psychological therapies in treating abnormality.

Biological therapies

Drugs

Drugs are the most widely used of all biological and psychological therapies. For some disorders, such as schizophrenia, drugs are the only generally available treatment. As we have learned more about the action of drugs, this has also helped in understanding the causes of psychological disorders.

Drugs used to treat schizophrenia and depression

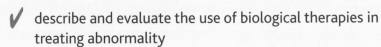
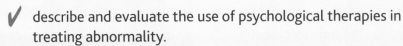

Schizophrenia
Drugs used in the treatment of schizophrenia are known as antipsychotics. These drugs work in the same way, by reducing the activity of the brain neurotransmitter dopamine. This supports the hypothesis that schizophrenia is caused by overactivity of dopamine pathways in the brain.

Depression
Drug therapies for depression can be highly effective. Widely used antidepressant drugs such as Prozac act by increasing the activity of the brain neurotransmitter serotonin. This supports the hypothesis that depression is linked to low levels of brain serotonin.

> **AQA Examiner's tip**
>
> The specification does not refer to particular drugs. However, the use of one or two examples is an effective way to demonstrate your understanding of their use in treating abnormality.

- Drugs are widely available and relatively cheap compared to psychological therapies. They can be extremely effective for conditions such as schizophrenia and anxiety, but do not work well for disorders such as phobias and eating disorders.
- Drugs can suppress symptoms but do not cure the disorder as they do not target the underlying causes. In schizophrenia, for example, drugs have to be taken for years in order to control the symptoms.
- All drugs used for psychological disorders have physiological and psychological side effects. Some, such as the anti-anxiety drugs Librium and Valium, can also lead to physical dependency.
- Drug treatment ignores any cognitive, emotional or environmental influences on the disorder. For some conditions, such as depression and anxiety, these influences can be central and should not be ignored.

> **AQA Examiner's tip**
>
> When evaluating therapies, students often focus on their limitations. Do not forget that all of the therapies also have positive features, in particular their effectiveness for specific conditions. Although not essential, this is an important part of evaluation.
>
> If the question involves a scenario, link your answer directly to the scenario.

■ Ethically there can be problems as people with schizophrenia or severe depression may not be capable of giving informed consent to the treatment.

Electroconvulsive therapy (ECT)

In ECT a small electric current is passed through the brain, producing an electrical convulsion similar to epilepsy. The behavioural signs are controlled by the use of anticonvulsant drugs, while the electrical discharge in the brain is thought to alter levels of brain neurotransmitters. Historically ECT was used for a wide range of conditions, including schizophrenia, but doubts about its effectiveness mean that in the UK it is now only prescribed for severe depression that has not responded to drugs or psychological therapies.

Evaluation

■ ECT is seen by some as a barbaric assault on the brain that is out of place in modern society. However, even though we do not know how it works, ECT has been shown to be effective in a number of patients with severe depression.

■ To be effective, a series of ECT treatments is given over a period of weeks. There is some evidence that this can lead to long-term memory problems in some patients.

■ Ethically it is doubtful if people with severe depression are capable of giving fully informed consent to this stressful and violent procedure.

Think about it

The use of ECT and, to a lesser extent, drugs can seem highly unethical. However, ECT is still used. Why should this be? Treating abnormality often requires a difficult balance between the ethical nature of a treatment and its potential effectiveness in relieving distressing conditions.

Psychological therapies

Therapies based on the psychodynamic approach

Psychoanalysis

Freud's psychoanalytic theory proposed that conflicts and fixations in childhood can result in adult psychological disorders. These conflicts and fixations are buried in the unconscious and are not accessible to the person's conscious awareness. Psychoanalytical therapy uses techniques to try to overcome the client's defence mechanisms and bring these unconscious issues into awareness so that they can be resolved.

Free association – the 'talking cure'

The client is encouraged to express anything that comes into their mind, perhaps a recent encounter with someone. Through free association of ideas one stream of thought leads to another, perhaps extending back into childhood.

During free association the therapist will be identifying key themes and ideas that can be analysed further during the therapeutic process.

Dream analysis

Freud referred to dreams as the 'royal road to the unconscious'. During dreams the usual ego defence mechanisms do not operate. Dreams reflect unconscious wishes and desires, usually originating from the id. Often they are too threatening to be consciously acknowledged so they are distorted into the imagery of the dream. So dreams have two levels:

- **Manifest content**: this is the imagery reported by the client.
- **Latent content**: this is the true meaning of the dream. It can be revealed by the therapist analysing the manifest content using Freud's techniques of dream interpretation.

Using free association and dream analysis the therapist can identify the conflicts underlying the client's anxieties and depression, and help the client resolve them.

Evaluation

- Because of its complex nature, psychoanalysis can be very long and expensive, lasting months or even years.
- The client has to be willing to undergo self-analysis and develop insights into their condition. Some people may not be willing to undergo this analytical process. In some disorders, such as schizophrenia, people may not have insight into their condition, and psychoanalysis would not be possible.
- Despite many critics, psychoanalysis has been shown to be an effective therapy for anxiety and depression.
- There can be ethical problems. Using free association and dream analysis to reveal traumatic events from childhood can lead to considerable distress, and clients may need long-term support to come to terms with such events.

Therapies associated with the behavioural approach

The behavioural approach assumes that all behaviour is learned. Therefore, to change abnormal behaviour we can use the learning principles outlined above.

Systematic desensitisation (SD)

The behavioural approach assumes that phobias are caused by the automatic response of fear becoming classically conditioned to particular objects or situations. SD is a form of counter-conditioning, where the therapist tries to replace the fear response by the alternative response of relaxation. So SD for a spider phobic might look like this.

Systematic desensitisation for a spider phobic

The client is asked to list situations from the most to the least feared, e.g. from a tarantula crawling over them to a picture of a small spider. The therapist then trains the client in deep relaxation techniques.	Once the client is comfortable at that level they are asked to imagine the next situation in the hierarchy, and the relaxation procedure is repeated.

The therapist asks the client to imagine the least feared situation while simultaneously doing their deep relaxation.

Over a series of sessions the client is counter-conditioned to associate relaxation with spiders rather than fear. They can stop at any time and go back to a less fearful level in the hierarchy, until eventually they can cope with the most feared situation.

Think about it

There are many books providing interpretations of dream imagery. How can we tell which interpretation, if any, is correct? That is the problem with Freud's psychoanalytic approach – it is impossible to test objectively and scientifically.

AQA Examiner's tip

If you have to evaluate psychoanalysis as part of an extended writing answer on therapies, make sure that you focus on the therapies and not on the psychodynamic approach in general. You will not earn many marks for mentioning neurotic Viennese women unless you link this directly to Freud's therapies.

Apply it

Think of a situation that you fear, e.g. heights. Write a short hierarchy of fear-arousing situations, from least to most frightening. Practice deep breathing and relaxation while you imagine yourself at the first stage, such as standing on a chair. There you have the basics of systematic desensitisation.

Flooding

Flooding is a more dramatic behavioural technique for phobias. It involves exposing the client to the feared stimulus, with no escape route. For instance, exposing them to real spiders in an enclosed space. The theory is that high levels of fear and anxiety cannot be sustained, but will reduce or extinguish. Flooding has been shown to be effective, but it is a highly stressful procedure.

Aversion therapy

This behavioural technique pairs a punishing stimulus with the undesirable behaviour. In the 1950s it was even used to try and 'cure' homosexuality, by pairing punishing electric shocks with pictures of naked men. There was no evidence that it ever worked. Today it is sometimes used as a therapy to reduce addictive behaviour. For example, smokers are given pills to make them feel sick whenever they smoke. The idea is that through classical conditioning the feeling of sickness is associated with smoking and should act to reduce smoking in the future.

Evaluation

- Behavioural therapies aim to change maladaptive learned associations. Therefore, they target symptoms rather than any underlying psychological or emotional causes of abnormality.

- However, systematic desensitisation can be extremely effective in the treatment of simple phobias, with success rates of 60–90 per cent.

- There is no evidence that behavioural therapies are effective in more complex disorders such as schizophrenia.

- There are serious ethical issues with flooding and aversion therapy, where clients experience intense fear and anxiety. Even with SD, the client has to visualise or experience fearful situations. Clients need to give fully informed consent and be given support after the therapy itself ends.

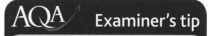

AQA Examiner's tip

Rather than simply listing a series of evaluative points, you should select the most relevant and explain why each is a strength or a limitation. You can then go on to explain the implications of the strength or limitation.

Therapies associated with the cognitive approach

The cognitive approach assumes that psychological disorders are caused by maladaptive and irrational perceptions and thoughts. Cognitive therapies aim to challenge and alter these irrational thoughts. Part of this approach also involves rewarding more effective and productive behaviours. Reward is part of the behavioural approach, so the therapy is usually referred to as cognitive-behavioural therapy (CBT).

Beck's cognitive therapy

Beck believes that depression is caused by negative schemata maintained by cognitive biases and pessimistic thoughts about the self, the world and the future. Beck's therapy aims to challenge these irrational cognitions and replace them with more realistic and optimistic thoughts.

Example of Beck's cognitive therapy

The therapist helps the client to identify key negative thoughts such as, 'I have always been bad at relationships'.

Diary keeping is an important part of this stage.

→

Using this material the therapist challenges these negative thoughts by identifying examples, however trivial, that contradict the client's own pessimistic views.

This is a form of reality testing, a key component of all cognitive behavioural therapies.

→

Behavioural techniques are used to encourage more positive behaviour. Small goals are set, such as talking casually to at least one new person a day. These minor achievements help a depressed person to develop a sense of personal effectiveness.

Evaluation

- CBT has been shown to be as effective as drug therapy for treating depression and anxiety. There is also evidence that the improvement may last longer.
- CBT assumes that the cause of depression, for example, lies in maladaptive thoughts, so it is targeting the causes of abnormality and not just the symptoms.
- Although effective for depression and anxiety disorders, CBT is less effective for phobias than systematic desensitisation, and severe disorders such as schizophrenia are not suited to CBT.
- The cognitive approach ignores genetic and biological factors in abnormality.
- Ethically, CBT avoids the in-depth probing associated with psychoanalysis. However, some people might find the diary keeping and self-monitoring associated with CBT stressful.
- The emphasis of CBT is on cognitive change or restructuring, and behavioural change without cognitive change is unlikely to help the depressed person.

AQA Examiner's tip

You may be given a description of a person with symptoms of some psychological disorder, and asked how they might be helped with e.g. CBT or psychoanalysis. Your answer must be focused on the person in the scenario. General answers on how CBT or psychoanalysis work will earn few marks.

Quick test questions

1 Which three of the following are associated with the failure to function adequately model of abnormality?

- [ ] Observer discomfort
- [ ] Aggression
- [ ] Unpredictability
- [ ] Maladaptiveness
- [ ] Depression

2 Which two of the following are characteristics of ideal mental health?

- [ ] Anxiety
- [ ] Being in touch with your feelings
- [ ] Calmness
- [ ] Resistance to stress
- [ ] Competitiveness

3 Which two of the following are assumptions of the biological model of abnormality?

- [ ] Abnormality is related to levels of brain neurotransmitters.
- [ ] Abnormality is caused by childhood stress.
- [ ] Abnormality is caused by faulty learning.
- [ ] Abnormality often has a genetic component.
- [ ] Abnormality is caused by maladaptive cognitions.

4 Which two of the following are assumptions of the psychodynamic model of abnormality?

- [ ] Abnormality is caused by faulty learning.
- [ ] Abnormality often has a genetic component.
- [ ] Abnormality can be caused by conflict between id, ego and superego.
- [ ] Abnormality can be related to fixation at the psychosexual stages of development.
- [ ] Abnormality is caused by maladaptive cognitions.

5 Which two of the following are assumptions of the behavioural model of abnormality?

- [ ] Abnormality often has a genetic component.
- [ ] Phobias can be caused by classical conditioning of fear to certain objects, animals or situations.
- [ ] Abnormality is caused by maladaptive cognitions.
- [ ] Eating disorders can be caused by observation of women in the media being rewarded for being thin.
- [ ] Abnormality is related to levels of brain neurotransmitters.

6 Which two of the following are assumptions of the cognitive model of abnormality?

- [ ] Abnormality is related to levels of brain neurotransmitters.
- [ ] Abnormality is caused by maladaptive thoughts and perceptions.
- [ ] Abnormality often has a genetic component.
- [ ] Negative schemata (ways of thinking) are maintained by cognitive biases such as maximisation and minimisation.
- [ ] Abnormality can be caused by conflict between id, ego and superego.

7 Which three of the following are characteristics of drug therapy for psychological disorders?

- [ ] It can be relatively quick and cheap.
- [ ] It can lead to physical and psychological dependence.
- [ ] It requires insight and self-analysis.
- [ ] It can have serious physical side effects.
- [ ] It requires a good client–therapist relationship.

8 Which three of the following are characteristics of systematic desensitisation?

- [ ] It treats causes, not symptoms.
- [ ] It treats symptoms, not causes.
- [ ] It is effective for all psychological disorders.
- [ ] It is effective mainly for phobias.
- [ ] It involves gradual exposure to the feared object or situation.

Exam-style questions

Marks available can range from 1 to 12. There are a variety of question styles that require you to use material differently. You must read each question carefully, follow the requirements and write enough to access the marks available.

Knowledge questions

1   Here are some important terms from the 'Individual differences (abnormality)' topic. Explain what is meant by each of these:

Deviation from social norms; Failure to function adequately; Deviation from ideal mental health; Biological approach; Psychodynamic approach; Cognitive approach; ECT; Psychoanalysis; Systematic desensitisation; Cognitive behavioural therapy

2   Explain one limitation of the deviation from ideal mental health definition of abnormality.   *(2 marks)*

3   Outline two features of the cognitive approach to psychopathology.
                                                   (2 marks + 2 marks)

4   Outline two definitions of abnormality.   *(3 marks + 3 marks)*

5   Outline key features of cognitive behavioural therapy.   *(3 marks)*

> **Apply it**
>
> Try writing 2-mark definitions for each of these terms. Now, develop your answer into a 3-mark definition. Remember that examples can be an effective method of elaborating an answer.

Application questions

1   Sally has a phobia of spiders. If she sees one she feels faint and giddy, and she will not go into some rooms in the house because she thinks there might be a spider there. She also avoids country walks as she thinks the grass will be full of spiders. Her family has persuaded her to see a behavioural therapist.

Explain how the therapist could use systematic desensitisation to help Sally with her spider phobia.   *(6 marks)*

> **AQA** **Examiner's tip**
>
> Six marks is equivalent to seven or eight minutes writing, so make sure that your answer covers the steps involved in SD – exposure to gradually more fear-provoking stimuli, combined with relaxation training at every stage. Demonstrate your understanding by using psychological terminology: classical conditioning, hierarchy of stimuli, counter-conditioning, etc. But stay focused on Sally.

2 Rory has been depressed for some time. He has no energy and often does not get up until the afternoon. He has lost his part-time job and has dropped out of his college course. He has lost touch with his closest friends.

Using one definition of abnormality, explain why Rory's behaviour might be seen as abnormal. *(3 marks)*

3 Karim has begun to suffer from social anxiety and now avoids social situations and meeting new people. This anxiety disorder is having a serious effect on his life, so Karim has seen his doctor who has recommended a course of anti-anxiety drugs. Karim is worried about taking drugs.

a What should the doctor tell Karim regarding problems associated with drug therapy for abnormality? *(3 marks)*

b Outline another therapy that might be used to help Karim. *(3 marks)*

> **AQA Examiner's tip**
>
> There is no set answer to question 2. Rory's behaviour could fit the deviation from social norms, or even more closely failure to function adequately or deviation from ideal mental health definitions of abnormality. Choose one model and show how two or three features can be mapped on to Rory's behaviour.

> **AQA Examiner's tip**
>
> Anti-anxiety drugs are particularly associated with side effects such as memory problems and tiredness. Dependence may also occur. Cognitive behavioural therapy might be an alternative therapy. Outline the features of CBT and why they might help Karim. Be brief, as only 3 marks are available.

> **AQA Examiner's tip**
>
> When you read through the scenario in application questions, underline key terms or phrases that cue you in to the requirements of the question.

Essay-style questions

1 Outline and evaluate the psychodynamic approach to psychopathology. *(12 marks)*

2 Discuss two or more definitions of abnormality. *(12 marks)*

3 Discuss the use of biological therapies in treating abnormality. *(10 marks)*

Sample answers

One way of defining abnormality is to see whether or not someone meets the criteria for ideal mental health. Marie has high self-esteem and a strong sense of identity.

(a) Describe two other criteria that you would expect Marie to display if she were psychologically healthy. *(2 marks + 2 marks)*

Criteria 1
She should be able to focus on the future and self-actualisation, to achieve her full potential.

Accurate point with an example

Criteria 2
She should have empathy, and be able to understand and be sympathetic to other people.

Again, accurate feature with some elaboration

(b) Outline one limitation of defining abnormality in terms of ideal mental health. *(2 marks)*

One limitation is that very few people have all six of the criteria for ideal mental health, so using this definition means that most people would be seen as abnormal.

The candidate has taken the sensible approach of identifying a limitation and then outlining the implication, so accessing both marks.

AQA   Examiner's comments

Although brief, each part is worth two marks. In each case an accurate point is made and elaborated. The candidate has demonstrated that they understand the point they are making, so they would achieve marks in the top band for each part.

Outline and evaluate the cognitive approach to psychopathology. *(12 marks)*

This approach says that abnormal behaviour is caused by problems in cognitive processes such as perception and thinking. Negative ways of thinking called schemata are maintained because the person has cognitive biases. For instance they maximise the bad things that happen and minimise the good things that happen to them. In this way they see themselves, the world and the future in a negative way. Beck called this the negative triad and used it to explain depression.

Good use of examples to demonstrate knowledge and understanding

The cognitive approach is good because it emphasises that abnormal behaviour is caused by cognitive processes in the brain. Research shows that people who are depressed recall more bad memories than people who are not depressed, because of their cognitive biases. So the cognitive approach is tackling the causes of abnormality rather than just the symptoms. However, the cognitive approach ignores biological and genetic factors in abnormality. Research has shown that depression is related to serotonin levels in the brain and twin studies show that there is also a genetic factor.

Excellent use of research evidence following a rather weak opening sentence

Again, effective use of research evidence to support the preceding evaluative point

The cognitive approach has also led to cognitive behavioural therapy, which tries to change people's negative thinking. This therapy is very effective for depression and so this supports the cognitive explanation of depression. However, it does not work for complicated conditions such as schizophrenia, and this is a limitation of the cognitive approach.

This might be just a limitation of the therapy. The jump to the approach is not convincing.

Another problem for the cognitive approach is that it does not explain where the negative schemata come from and it is difficult anyway to define what schemata are.

AQA   Examiner's comments

A concise answer but there is very little irrelevant material. The outline of the cognitive approach is slightly limited, e.g. little detail of schemata or cognitive biases, but generally quite clear and informed. However, there are four or five good evaluative points, in some cases supported by research evidence. Examples of disorders such as depression and schizophrenia are used effectively. Although these disorders are not listed in the Specification, accurate and relevant psychological knowledge will always earn marks. Reference to therapy earns some credit, although it is important not to see therapy and approach as the same thing. The whole answer demonstrates clear understanding. AO1 generally accurate, low end of top band marks; AO2 informed, high end of top band marks.

Index